WELSH BORDER WITCHCRAFT
A RENDITION OF THE OCCULT HISTORY OF THE WELSH MARCH

WELSH BORDER WITCHCRAFT

A RENDITION OF THE OCCULT HISTORY OF THE WELSH MARCH

Gary St. M. Nottingham

Published by Avalonia

Published by Avalonia

BM Avalonia
London
WC1N 3XX
England, UK
www.avaloniabooks.co.uk

WELSH BORDER WITCHCRAFT

First Edition 2018.

ISBN 978-1-910191-11-8

Cover Sigil - The Shropshire Magazine, 1952, originating from Robert Cross Smith's The Straggling Astrologer, 1820.

Design by Satori, for Avalonia.

British Library Cataloguing in Publication Data. A catalogue record for this book is available from the British Library.

Shropshire Nursery Rhyme

..... and when the pricking time did tell
the finder came from fiery hell
to rid this earth of monstrous beasts
and lay them down for the devil's feasts

And now a ghoul he wanders still
to find the child that bears him ill
for Gideon Planke will find you out
for he is coming.... have no doubt!

Gideon Planke, Witchfinder,
South Shropshire 1648

Table of Contents

CHAPTER ONE

A Bloody Landscape

For most people in the U.K., Mid Wales and its border with England will be somewhere vague, a landscape largely unknown and barely considered. Ask where Shropshire is, or Hereford, or indeed the old Welsh counties of Montgomeryshire or Radnorshire and most people will not know. Yet this area, known as the Welsh March, has in the past played an important part in the history of these islands, and has also been a repository of the esoteric and the occult. While many people, both those in the occult community and the wider public, are unfamiliar with this, this work endeavours to address this situation.

The landscape of the Welsh March is an area that was defined in the years after the Norman Conquest; although King Offa, the 8th century Mercian, had created the dyke named after him in an attempt to bring clarity and order to the area. However, over the centuries struggle for possession of the landscape became a battlefield between the Norman Marcher lords and the Welsh princes. Carved out by bloodshed, cunning and treachery it is a land heavy with the numinous and redolent of the spirit of Merlin. It is both remote and secretive, and despite modern communication is yet in many ways still isolated from the mainstream of life. The old Welsh counties of Brecon, Montgomery and Radnor now form the modern Welsh county of Powys, a name taken from the old Celtic kingdom of that name which was centred on the Roman town of Viroconium in Shropshire. On the English side of the border the counties of Hereford and Shropshire still bear witness to the scars caused by the conflicts of the past. Where England meets Wales the two countries merge in a welter of castles, hillforts and river valleys, symbols of the populace's determination to hold on to that which they had at any cost.

Curiously, there are various alignments within the landscape created by stone circles, standing stones and old churches. Alignments which mark out a sacred landscape and acknowledge the solar year. One example can be seen around the border town of Clun in southwest Shropshire. Here, exactly four and half miles from its castle, dominating the bend in the river, are five churches which create a pentagram in the landscape. And over this setting are various alignments which mark both the longest and shortest days' sunrises and sunsets; a veritable unknown solar temple in the landscape.

Travelling south and over the border into Radnorshire, the largest woodhenge in Europe was discovered in the locality of the 'Radnorshire Basin' during the 1990's. This incredible structure covered seventy acres and was created from four thousand oak trees, each oak pillar weighing four tons - yet it is barely known.

And then there's the Dinedor Serpent a quartz pathway which was uncovered when the Hereford council was creating a new road around the eastern side of Hereford. It ran from the hill fort on nearby Dinedor hill to the banks of the river Wye. The 'experts' were puzzled by this construction as the stone was too soft to be a road, and then in the moonlight, they were amazed at its beauty as it shone and sparkled in the soft Luna glow. What no doubt was an archaeological treasure was promptly covered over, and the new road driven over it.

The idea of a ceremonial pathway may also be the explanation of the story of how a dragon is trapped in the landscape of the nearby Radnor forest. This bleak mountainous landscape, not far from the Radnor basin and its woodhenge, is surrounded by a circle of Saint Michael churches, if one should fail then the dragon escapes.

One cannot but consider whether the dragon legend is a reference to a similar ceremonial path to that at Dinedor hill, which is a mere broomstick ride away. This landscape and the myth is explored in Phil Rickman's highly readable novel *The Crown of Lights*.

The landscape is truly sacred. But who are its people?

Most of Shropshire and eastern Mid Wales were once part of the kingdom of the Cornovii, a Celtic tribe who quickly became 'Romanized.' They were the only Celtic tribe trusted enough to help Rome in the administration of the newly conquered lands of Britannia. Their tribal capital of Viroconium became the fourth largest town in Roman Britain and also the haunt of the Pelagian Christians who (among their other heresies) declared that Jesus was merely a man, and not God incarnate.

The author Graham Phillips makes a compelling case for Viroconium being the original Camelot and Arthur of legend being based here, because the town survived for several decades as a Roman town after much of the country had been conquered by the invading Saxon tribes. In time the Angles dominated northern Shropshire, while the Saxon tribe the Magonsaete, who had arrived in Herefordshire, colonised south Shropshire as far north as modern Shrewsbury.

As the River Severn flowed out of Wales it became the boundary between two very different Shropshires: the north, flat and fen like, and the south with its secret valleys and wooded hilltops; the contrasts are quite marked.

Hereford, a soft and rich county, with its hop-yards, orchards and deep red soil, is home to the stalwart Hereford cattle, and had, like Shropshire, been vulnerable to Welsh raiders, whose scant economy was supported by what they could take from the English villages along the border. Both counties make Mid Wales, with its bleakness and lonely hilltops, its thin soils and empty spaces, seem like a lost land. Yet despite the bloodshed over the centuries the intermarriage between the inhabitants of both sides of the border, the struggle for the land, and the need to coax its yield, has produced an indigenous populace who are neither English nor Welsh and who while aware of the outside world, are not of it.

CHAPTER TWO

Of Cunning Men & Women

'Dunna I snare souls like conies
En cure warts en the chin cough?'
Wizard Beguildy
'Precious Bane', Mary Webb

While some accounts of the practices and charms used by local conjurors have survived, it is curious how they have faded from local memory so quickly. In many areas, there would have been somebody with a rudimentary knowledge of herbal plants and their properties, with some people having a basic astrological expertise and perhaps access to a simple magical tradition, yet there were those too who had fuller ingress to the magical traditions of the West. Those who had a magical interest, and were from the higher echelons of society, were in a more fortunate position than ordinary people - who also studied what they could and when they could of the magical traditions. Being freed from the restraints of everyday living, wealthy magical practitioners were in a privileged position. Yet it was the poor practitioners whose knowledge was often a real benefit to their local communities.

As a result, there appeared two types of magical practitioners who could be found in the area. There were those of the conjuror class, that is people of either sex, from the working population, and who would use their knowledge for the benefit of the community; and there were those of the educated classes who used their abilities to further their own interests and understandings of such matters. Both classes of practitioner were apparent on the border. For many there was nobody to turn to in times of trouble; one's livestock could quite easily be the family's life savings. With no safety net, when death or disaster struck there was often nowhere to go for help. Yet the conjuror would often do their best to invoke supernatural aid on behalf of their clients, perform acts of divination, or lift the runs of bad luck or curses, and who would provide what help they could to aid the well-being of the family and their livestock. However, the influence of two world wars and the resulting upheaval of the populations - and of course the complex industrialisation of modern times - must have played a significant role in the demise of this forgotten part of our social history.

While we consider it to be no more than rural superstition and a lack of scientific knowledge which created the demand for the conjuror, it can be demonstrated that they were still in demand up to the beginning of the last century, and in some instances up to and including the war years. And it was not merely the rural population who required their services: many could also be found in the urban environments, providing charms for everyday problems.

While cunning folk and conjurors abounded and were in reach of most of society, it must be noted that it was not only the illiterate and the poor who consulted with them. Often members of the local elite, landowners and other members of the establishment, would also frequent their company. This can be attested to by reference to the trial of William Davies for the murder of Nanny Morgan of Much Wenlock in 1857. The practitioners of the arte were often, but not always, at the edge of society, frequently being characters the local populace were wary of and didn't like to offend.

Some conjurors would use their reputations to cower individuals into doing their bidding, keeping an 'arcane potency' about themselves and displaying the mysteries in their homes to impress any prospective clientele. The herbs hanging out to dry, odd-looking curios, books and semi-occult paraphernalia were no doubt suggestive to those who saw them displayed in dimly-lit rooms. However, not all conjurors and cunning folk were benevolent, and some were without a doubt positively criminal, as they cheated and duped the credulous. Others were a real benefit to their communities and practised their arte generally for the good of all. An interesting and clear account of a conjuror and their activities is amply detailed in Mary Webb's novel 'Precious Bane' which she set in 19th century Shropshire; featuring her characters the wizard Beguildy, the Cunning Man, and Caster of the Planets.

Webb depicts a conjuror as being typically one who is versed in his arte as he played half confidence trickster, but one also who trafficks with the spirits of other realms. Cunning folk and conjurors were expected to be able to turn their skills to making charms and to have sufficient herbal knowledge for the treatment of a wide range of complaints. They were also expected to be able to find lost objects or people who had gone missing. Sometimes they were called upon to detect stolen property and the thief, and to punish them accordingly.

In Charlotte Burne's work *'Shropshire Folklore'*, published in 1883, she gives an account of a Ludlow conjuror who was consulted by the police for the detection of a theft. The story tells how he walked down Corve Street with his divining rod which indicated the house where the thief was residing. On being approached by the police the man confessed that he had been responsible for the crime and was apprehended accordingly. Various accounts have survived which indicate that conjurors and cunning folk were numerous both throughout the 19th century and the preceding two. Many built up large practices in the locality where they dwelt. Mainly this was done through word of mouth, although they also advertised with the publishing of handbills and pamphlets.

This can be seen with the practice of Thomas Parkins who, while dwelling in Lincolnshire, used the services of a Hereford umbrella maker to promote his craft. Some adopted the title of Dr or implied they had acquired an education in the arte from a known authoritative source. Others claimed that they had received instruction from the angels and spirits of God. For some their arte was their main source of income, many had however regular employment and were small-time trades people or farmers. They could also be found among the professional classes. In 1634, Richard Napier, the rector of Lindford, Buckinghamshire, was noted by his parishioners for his astrological skills and his ability to lift curses and bad luck. This he claimed was part of his Christian ministry, and by his arte he had brought much healing to those who were troubled in both mind, body and spirit. He would often use the altar as his working table when casting horoscopes. In 1540 the steward of Elfael, an old kingdom in the south-west corner of

Radnorshire, complained that the vicar of Aberderw charmed sick animals and people. The cleric, it was said, would place written charms which had been sprinkled with holy water over the doors of barns and buildings. He would often, when required, hang charms around the necks of children for their protection and wellbeing.

Charmers and conjurors were primarily consulted in matters concerning protection from misfortune, although they could and often did perform other services. Their popularity was ensured with the persecution of Roman Catholicism at the Reformation, as many charms and magical workings would have been performed by a Catholic priest within a Catholic setting. With the rise of the conjuror came a demand for the written occult word on a large scale.

Despite the witchcraft persecutions of the 17th century this was an important time for the publication of occult texts in England. Several grimoires or grammars of magic were translated into English from Latin, and these were made available by various booksellers and publishers of the time.

For example, the Heptameron, a 13th century grimoire which gave concise instruction on the conjuration of spirits, was translated into English for the first time. This work was devoured by the occult reading public which created a demand for the publishers to which they duly attended. Other works such as Agrippa's *'Three Books of Occult Philosophy'* as well as his fourth book, sometimes attributed to his pupil Werius, were studied and put to use by the conjurors of the time. Despite what we consider to be the lack of communications, compared to the standard we are used to today, it is surprising how these people were in contact with one another, exchanging ideas and purchasing books. For example, the 18th-century bookseller Lackington and Allen offered 150 occult titles to the public, and Paul Kleber Monad, writing in his work *'Solomon's Secret Arts'* considers how during this time a Herefordshire alchemist arranges for an athanor (alchemical furnace) to be made and shipped over to him from Paris! Such accounts make it quite clear that the lack of modern communications was no barrier to the students of the arte.

Yet the most popular work was the 16th-century *'Discoverie of Witchcraft'* by the Kentish squire and J.P. Reginald Scott. In 1580 he published his book on witchcraft as an endeavour to prove it was all fake. However, he had collected such a lot of information from the practitioners in his area that it became the standard reference book of its time! Which somewhat defeated the object, particularly as it was reprinted eight times in quick succession.

It is clear the charms which were displayed in work were being used in Radnorshire and Montgomeryshire until recent times, with several being found hidden in old buildings. Therefore, not only had Elizabethan witchcraft charms found their way into Mid Wales and the border, they were still being used among the farming community to protect livestock up to and including the 20th century. Other favourite texts were Culpeper's *Complete Herbal* and the astrological writings of the 17th-century astrologer William Lilly, who predicted the Great Fire of London twelve years before it happened.

Although such works as *The Illustrated Occult Sciences'* by Ebenezer Sibley, published at the end of the 18th-century, were also highly influential, two occult magazines that appeared during the early half of the 19th century, *The Straggling Astrologer* and *The Familiar Astrologer* were also in keen demand.

Both these publications gave explicit occult instruction on a wide variety of magical practices and were avidly read by the conjurors and the students of the arte. But it was the publishing in 1801 of Francis Barrett's work *'The Magus'* or *'The Celestial Intelligencer'* which granted ingress for many into the occult world. Barrett had done what no other had done previously. He had taken the more relevant information from several earlier and rare occult works and had made them available for all. His compendium of charms and grimoire material proved to be an instant success. At this time John Denley, the Covent Garden occult bookseller, also published a variant of the *'Key of Solomon'*, a 16th-century grimoire based upon earlier works. It was so sought after that the price rose quickly to £20 a copy! This when agricultural wages were eight shillings a week or forty pence in today's money. And demand for the work was high demonstrating an avid readership for such material.

Not only can we assume that people were paying a high price for the skills of the conjuror, but also that there was a reasonably educated sector among the more inquisitive members of the working class feeding the demand for such works and challenging some prevailing attitudes that the working classes rarely received any education. Some were fortunate that they had received a basic understanding of the three R's, arithmetic, reading and writing.

These became essential skills for a conjuror who needed to impress prospective clients that they had access to arcane knowledge which they could command should they choose to do so. At a time when there was no health service, and ordinary people had no real redress in law, with the clergy also being so remote from their flock, it is not hard to see how the conjurors supplied a real and much-needed service in their communities. Despite being attacked by clerics and the social commentators of the day, for many, there was nobody else to turn to in their hour of need.

It was common among 17th-century English ritual magicians to claim some ancestry or connection with Wales, as the country was seen to be a land where magic of all types was practised. This was a point previously noted by the 12th-century Welsh cleric Geraldus Cambrensis or Gerald of Wales. Sometimes the use of the Welsh language and terminology was used in charms. This can be seen with the prosecution of Margaret Blunt in 1528 for the practice of witchcraft. She claimed that she could cure agues, lameness, lift curses and alleviate bad luck. The prayers which she used had to be recited in Welsh, and they had been taught to her by an elderly Welsh woman who was known as 'Old Mother Emet.'

Conjurors in Wales were known as 'dyn hysbys', or wise-men, and I was informed by an assistant at Aberystwyth Museum that he personally knew of local farmers approaching the surviving dyn hysbys for charms to protect their farms, "because that was what they did."

However, as far as possible this act was always done in secret, not for any implied magical advantage but basically because they did not want their neighbours to know they believed in such things. This approach is clearly illustrated in Elizabeth Clarke's biographical account of her childhood on a Radnorshire smallholding in the 1930's where she says

> '...*meeting neighbours on a certain road, it was easy to guess where they were going – they had a guilty look. And they were regularly to be seen because some documents had to be renewed every year, when the potency of spells was said to have evaporated.*
>
> *Superstition was far from dead in my childhood. Its symbols and portents were lightly talked about, but its practice was kept out of sight like secret drinking...*'

CHAPTER THREE

At The Sign Of The Cross

'En if I curse en they be cursed'
Wizard Beguildy
'Precious Bane', Mary Webb

The charms which have survived are, without exception, based upon Christian sources and written material. Apart from Margaret Blunt there is no Welsh terminology used in the charms, even though Welsh was the common language particularly among the farming communities on both sides of the border, and still is within the Welsh hinterlands. All the charms are in English with some Hebrew, Kabbalistic and Latin terminology. The use of Gnostic aspects is also apparent, as is astrological terminology and cyphers. The use of the Abracadabra formula is a clear, if not appreciated, borrowing from the 2nd century CE Gnostic magical praxis.

Of the charms and magical workings which have survived it is clear that not all were for a benign outcome. Some were to create misfortune in the victim's life and this can be quite clearly seen from three curses which were found in three separate places and are displayed in the Hereford museum. One curse is a knitted poppet, a doll, with a plait of the victim's hair woven into it and put to nefarious use. It was found in East Street, Hereford and has been dated as late as the 19th century. It was found with the following conjuration:

'...Mary Ann Ward
I act this spell upon you with my holl heart
Wishing you to never rest nor to eat nor to sleep the resten of your life
I hope your flesh will waste away and I hope you will never spend
another penny I ought to have wishing this from my whole heart...'

THE HEREFORD POPPET
(HEREFORD MUSEUM)

A second curse was a figure which had been carved from wood and placed in a coffin. This was found walled up in a house at Woolhope in 1987. The figure is pinned to the back of the coffin with a nail, perhaps with the deliberate symbolic intent of no escape.

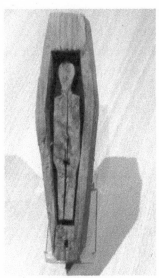

POPPET IN COFFIN
(HEREFORD MUSEUM)

The third curse which is displayed in the Hereford museum was found under the floorboards of a chemist's shop in St Peter's Square. The figure consists of two playing cards, one the knave of diamonds and the other a spade. A ball of hair is impaled with an iron nail and a wood splinter. It is then tied with a length of cord. Beneath this is a refreshment card with the name of the individual written upon it, which one may assume is the victim of the act. There is also a date, 7th August 1861, written on the card.

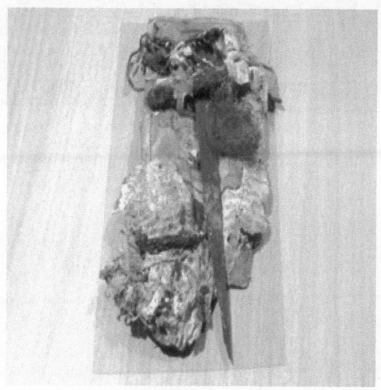

HAIR CHARM
(HEREFORD MUSEUM)

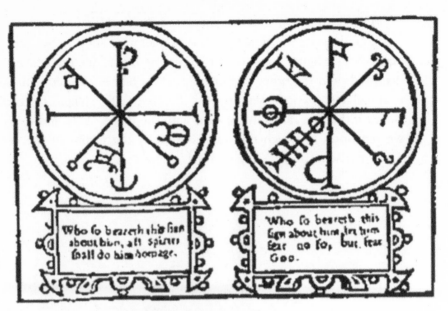

SEALS FROM THE DISCOVERIE OF WITCHCRAFT.

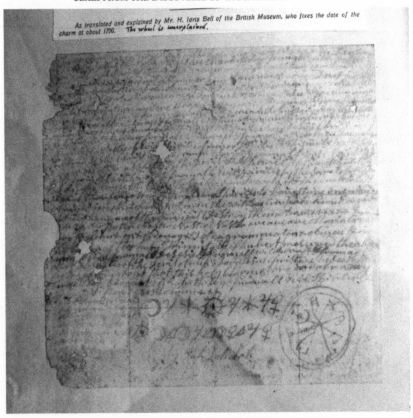

CHARM FOUND AT ST MICHAEL'S CHURCH

CASCOB, RADNORSHIRE

In the bottom left hand corner is the Abracadabra charm written as tradition demands:

ABRACADABRA
ABRACADABR
ABRACADAB
ABRACADA
ABRACAD
ABRACA
ABRAC
ABRA
ABR
AB
A

The seal on the right is the one that is used on the Cascob charm and others found in the locality. The charm contains the following wording…

> '…In the name of the Father, Sun & of the Holy Ghost Amen X X X and in the name of the Lord Jesus Christ I will delive (relieve) Elizabeth Loyd from all witchcraft and from all Evil spirites & from all evil men or Women or Wizardes or hardness of hart Amen X X X
>
> and into that universal nature God will interpose Himself against skill diabolical Amen X X X [Psalm XLIV, 1] He raised up my heart, I indite a good matter touching the King. O Lord open Thou my lips & my tongue shall shew forth Thy praise, to turn aside the grasp of the wicked and malignant. Lord Jesus Christ Saviour of mankind I beseech the preserver of Elizabeth Loodyd from all witchcraft evil men or women & from all spirites or wizardes or hardnes of hart. Amen X X X
>
> & this I will trust in the Lord Jesus Christ my Readeemer and Saviour from all witchcraft and from all other men or women & from all assaltes of evil spirities of men or deviles & this I will trust in the Lord Jesus Christ my Redeemer & Saviour from all Evil Spirites & from all other assaltes of the Devil and that he Relive Elizabeth Loyd from all witchcraft and from all evil spirites by the same apower as he deid cause the blind to see, the lame to walke & the dum to

talke & that thou findest with unclean spirits to be in thire one mindes Amen X X X as willeth Jehovah Amen. the witches compassed her abought but in the name of the Lord i will destroy them Amen X X X X X X X

pater pater pater Noster Noster Noster ave ave ave Maria Creed ro paclorn in saecula seculorum X on X Adonay X Tetragrammaton Jehovah X Amen & in the name of the Holy Trinnity & of Hubert preserved the above mind and body from all Desesis & from all witchcraft & from all assaltes of the Devil, Amen. O Lord Jesus Christ we beseeth thee for thy mercy grant that this holy charm ABRACADABRA may cure thy survant Elizabeth Loyd from all Evil Spirites and from all ther desesis Amen X X X by JAH JAH JAH

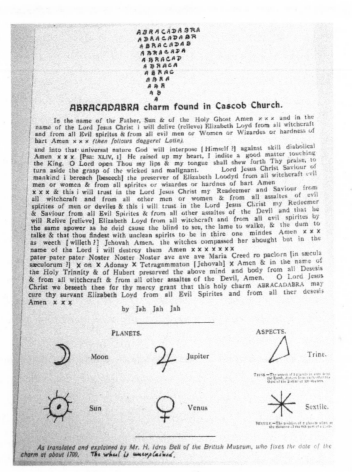

MODERN COPY OF THE CASCOB CHARM

This surviving example of a conjuror's charm, which uses aspects of the Christian ritual as well as astrological symbology, a talismanic figure from Scott's *Discoverie of Witchcraft*,' and a 2nd-century occult charm, can be seen at the church of St. Michael, Cascob, near Knighton in Radnorshire. This charm has to my knowledge been found at various other places in the locality, with several original charms being held by the National Library of Wales at Aberystwyth.

The church of St. Michael is a curious place at the end of a secret valley which runs into the foothills of Radnor Forest, yet here is probably one of the finest examples of the conjuror's arte on display. On the wall in the church is the original charm that was found many years ago in the churchyard. It was created for Elizabeth Lloyd and was used to overcome all witchcraft and evil spirits. It is in English and no Welsh is used. Whilst it has been dated to the early 18th century, in my opinion, this is wrong, and I consider it to have been likely created after 1825. An identical charm was found at Pentrenant, near Churchstoke in Montgomeryshire, and is on display at Welshpool Museum, with the suggestion that it is from the design of the Pope's ring. In my view however this observation is wrong, as it is clearly from the work of Reginald Scott.

I would suggest that the material for this charm came from two sources. Firstly the wheel design is quite clearly from Reginald Scott's work, previously mentioned, and the Abracadabra formula is taken from either the '*Straggling Astrologer*' or '*The Astrologer of the Nineteenth Century*'. Both were occult magazines published by Robert Cross Smith in 1825. Cross Smith (1795-1832), who wrote under the name Raphael, was during his short life highly influential upon the conjurors of the day with his magazines. Despite no internet or modern-day postal service, this publication was reaching all parts of the country, via peddlers and travelling salesmen. The use of the Abracadabra formula was first recorded by Quintus Serenus Sammonicus, who was a doctor to the Roman Emperor Severus during his expedition to Britain in 208CE. He considered that it would cure fever if it was written as a decreasing word and hung around the patient's neck. That it was still being used in mid-Wales nearly two thousand years later attests perhaps to its efficacy?

Cross Smith, who made the charm available to the conjurors, claimed that he had received it from an occult group called the Mercurii, and that the charm itself was from the 12th century, although he doesn't name his source for this. However, it is quite clearly older than this by at least a thousand years. He says that for the charm to work it must be written as a pyramid on virgin parchment, with the quill of a raven and the ink formed from the soot of a consecrated wax candle. The charm must be created when the moon is in either Sagittarius or Pisces, both astrological signs being ruled by Jupiter, a benevolent planet. If this cannot be done then the full moon may be used instead.

The charm must be worn around the neck for one lunar month. As the moon travels through all the signs of the zodiac in one month the charm is worn from where the moon starts her journey until she returns to the same point. For the charm to work it was deemed necessary for the wearer to have faith in God, and when creating it, the following oration had to be said (and in complicated cases repeated daily)....

> '...O Sweet Lord Jesus Christ ✝ the true God, who didst descend
> from the kingdom of thy Almighty Father being sent
> to wash away our sins, to release those who were in prison
> and afflicted, to console the sorrowful and the needy,
> to absolve and to liberate me, thy servant,
> from my affliction and tribulation, in which I am placed.
> So, O, Omnipotent Father, thou didst receive us again
> by his expiation, into that paradise, by thy blood, O Jesu ✝
> obtained and didst make us equal among and angels and men.
> Thou O Lord Jesus Christ ✝ wert worthy to stand between
> me and mine enemies and to establish my peace and to show
> thy grace unto me, and to pour out thy mercy.
> And thou O Lord didst extinguish the anger of my enemies which
> they contained against me, as thou didst take away the wrath of
> Esau which he had against Jacob, his brother.
> O Lord Jesus ✝ extend thine arm towards me and deliver me from
> my affliction even as thou didst deliver Abraham from the hands of

the Chaldean and his son Isaac, from the sacrifice, and Jacob from the hand of his brethren; Noah from the deluge; and even as thou didst deliver thy servant Lot, thy servants Moses and Aaron and thy people Israel from the hands of Pharoah and out of the lands of Egypt. David from the hands of Saul and the giant Goliath, or as thou delivered Susannah from her accusers; Judith from the hands of Holofernes, Daniel from the den of the lions, the three youths from the fiery furnace; Jonah from the whale's belly, or as thou delivered the son of Cannanea, who was tormented by the devil,

even as thou delivered Adam from hell, by thou most precious blood, and Peter and Paul from chains. So, O most sweet Lord Jesus ✦ Son of the Living God, preserve me thy servant from my affliction, and mine enemies, and be mine assistant and my blessing. By thy holy incarnation by thy fasting and thirst by thy labours and affliction, by thy stripes by thy thorny crown by thy drink of gall and vinegar, by thy most cruel death, by the words which thou spakest upon the cross, by thy descent into hell, by thy consolation of thy disciples by thy wonderful ascension by the great gifts and by the holy names,

Adonay ✦ Eloym ✦ Heloym ✦ Yacy ✦ Zazael ✦
Paliel ✦ Saday ✦ Yzoe ✦ Yaras ✦ Caelphi ✦ Saday ✦
and by thy ineffable name יהוה *Jehovah ✦*

By all these holy omnipotent and all-powerful names of singular efficacy and extraordinary power, which the elements obey, and at which the devils tremble: O most gracious **Jesu** ✦ *grant I beseech thee that this holy charm which I now wear about my person may be the means of healing my lamentable sickness,*

so shall the praise thereof be ascribed O Lord to thee alone,

and thou alone shall have all the glory.' **Amen.** *Fiat Fiat Fiat*

In his account of working this charm Robert Cross Smith remarks that the charm can be worked without the person being present simply by scraping out a line of the charm with a new knife and doing this daily until the text is wiped out. As this is done the following is said…

'So, as I destroy the letters of this charm Abracadabra,

So, by virtue of this sacred name may all grief and dolor

depart from (name of person) in the name of the Father, and of the Son, and of the Holy Ghost. In the name of the Father I destroy this disease. In the name of the Son I destroy this disease, and in the name of the Holy Spirit I destroy this disease. Amen.'

The combining of the 2nd-century Abracadabra charm with the talismanic design from 16th-century Scott's work shows, I feel, some ingenium - somebody had created a new spell from two old ones and then invoked various aspects of Christian cosmology. In many ways, one can see a similarity with the Hoodoo practices of the southern States of America, where biblical terminology becomes apparent within the spell work of the practitioner. For many people reading material was generally limited, compared to today, but most people would have had some familiarity with the bible and would know of its stories and characters. Thus they had an emotional connection to them which could be subsequently exploited as 'Names of Power' in spell workings.

The 'Hubert' mentioned in the charm is perhaps St Hubert, also known as Hubertus, a 7th-century saint who was the patron of hunters, mathematicians, opticians and metalworkers. He was considered of noble birth and to be a keen huntsman, who was converted to Christianity after he encountered a white stag that bore a crucifix between his antlers and who spoke to him. With his association with hunting dogs, he was often petitioned for the cure of rabies. The language is a mixture of Roman Catholicism, as seen by the use of the terms Pater Noster and the Ave Maria, both no doubt ecclesiastical concepts that were left over from the Reformation and long abandoned by the Anglican church. With the use of astrological symbology, such as the planetary symbols, and the signs for such aspects as sextiles and trines, one could assume that the creator of the charm was conversant with their meaning. But this may not be so as they could have been merely copying a set formula.

In 1970 Ida Gandy, a doctor's wife from the nearby Clun valley in south-west Shropshire, wrote in her book *'Idler on the Shropshire Borders'*, an account of local life, how she visited Cascob on May Day 1952. Walking from south Shropshire to see the charm of which she had heard, she was surprised to see that rowan crosses were tied to the stable doors on the local farms. When she asked about the practice she was told that it was done to keep the fairies away from the farms.

The Cascob charm has been found at various places within Mid Wales and the border, suggestive of a local tradition among the farming families. One variant was discovered during a barn renovation in 1985 at Bishop's Castle, south-west Shropshire. When the farmer took the charm to the local museum, they, after telling him what it was, wanted it for their collections. The farmer was adamant that it was going back to the farm to be re-interred in the barn where it had been discovered.

A second charm was found in the Bishop's Castle area on a farm at Pentrenant in 1909, hidden under a feed trough in a barn. It is now on display at Welshpool museum in mid-Wales and follows the same formula as the Cascob charm. The charm declares that it was made for William Bains and the inscription reads....

'... In the name of the father and of the son and of the Holy Gost Amen XXX
And in the name of the Lord Jesus Christ his redeemer and saviour he will relieve William Bains Pentrynant entreat his cows, calves, milk, butter, cattle of all ages, mares, horses of all ages
Sheep, yews (ewes) lambes, pigs, sowes, and prosper him in all his farm and from all witchcraft and all deseases Amen XXX
Gasper fert myrham thus melchor Balthazar auraum hec tria quregum salvatis a morbo a Christ pietate ea duco Amen XXX
In educto unversanilam amathuram – positis sarah adversus artedovalis Amen XXX
Eructavit cor meaum verbum bonum dicam cuncta opera meregi
Domino labia mea aperies and os meun annutiabit verbatim cunctre brachna iniquet lingua malusqua subverted a Lord Jesus Christ homnoum he hereth the preserver of William Pentrynant his cows calves milk butter cattle of all ages mares sucklers horses of all ages yews lambes sheep of all ages piges sowes and prosper him on this farm to liv luckly saved from all witchcraft and evil men or women or spirits or wizards or hardness of hart Amen XXX
And this I will trust in the Lord Jesus Christ my redeemer and saviour he will relive William Bains Pentrynant his cows calves milk

butter cattle of all ages piges sowes and everything that is his possession to live lucken and proster him on this farm and (saved) from all witchcraft by the same power as he did cause the blind to see the lame to walk and the dum to talk and thou findest with unclean spirits as wilt Jehovah Amen XXX the witch compassed him about but the Lord will destroy them all pater pater pater

Noster noster noster ave ave ave maria creed car acetum X on X adona X tetragra Amen XXX and in the name of the holy trinity preserve all the above named from evil deseases whatsoever

Amen X...'

As with the Cascob charm, the Pentrenant charm uses no Welsh language, but there is liberal use of Kabbalistic terminology. Apart from the vagaries of the wording, the meaning is quite clear: it is a charm offering protection to the farm and its livestock, keeping them safe from all harm and malefic intent. It is a medley of prayer, spell and magical enchantment. The individual who created the charm has drawn heavily upon biblical imagery and script, which in turn serve as the 'Words of Power.'

There are also recognisable Latin phrases used within the charm which have been taken from the psalms and among the words of power is the Latin phrase *'Caro factus est'*, *'He was made flesh.'*

The use of 'Dog Latin' is not uncommon among the conjurors and is suggestive of a written tradition that has been preserved. It contained the familiar seal from Scott in the lower right-hand corner of the charm, this being something which all the charms have in common.

Writing in his work *'Archaeology of Ritual Magic'* Ralph Merrifield observes that the paper which the charm had been written on was of a type that was common just before the First World War, thus dating it to about the Edwardian era.

This is, therefore, something which would have been created some 50-80 years after the Cascob charm, which now supports a premise that a tradition was being preserved in the locality. Someone would have had to inherit the means of producing these charms, thus suggesting a local written tradition. This is supported by the experience of an eminent Welsh historian living in Mid Wales, who told me that he knew a local farmer's wife who had once told him how her family had always made charms for their neighbours. Having been given a charm by her he kept it in his study, but embarrassingly he had to admit that for some strange reason it was never where he left it last, and he would always have to wait for it to turn up!

I was shown the charm, when it was eventually found, and, having seen it, can say that it is the same as the one at Cascob. Therefore, I feel that it is reasonable to conclude that there is a tradition in Mid Wales and its border country of a magical practice that has been passed on within the locality among certain families for at least two hundred years. This has been unrecognised and unknown by the wider magical community. When considering the Abracadabra formula, we can see a tradition whereby the conjurors have perhaps unknowingly been working with material that can be quite easily traced back two thousand years. Furthermore, it can be concluded that the conjuror has been drawing upon a pre-Christian formula, one that has been quite clearly used in the classical world, and among the magical workers thereof.

In 1918, when a farm was sold at Devil's Bridge, Dyfed, a version of this charm was found in a stable, which had been used to cure a sick mare. This charm is now in the care of the National Library of Wales. Several charms all written by the same hand have been found among the farming community and are deposited in the archives of Aberystwyth, Bangor University and the National Folk Museum of Wales at Cardiff. They were created between the war years and again indicate a local tradition which has survived.

One charm which was found at Aberhafesp, near Newtown, Montgomeryshire, and is also in the collections of the National Library of Wales, was used to protect a pig. It was found buried in the wall of a pigsty and was inscribed with the following incantation...

+ Lignum Sanctae Cruis defendat me a malis presentibus
Preateritus et futuris Interior
Bus et ++ William J----- +++
Omnes spiritus laudet Dominun Mosen habent et prophetas

Exurget Deus et disipenture inimci essus

'…The wood of the Holy Cross, defend me from all evils
Present, past and future, within and without ✛✛
William J ✛✛
Let every spirit praise the Lord they have Moses and the prophets.
Let God arise and his enemies be scattered…'

A 19th-century conjuror and farmer from Llan y Blodwell, a small village near Oswestry, was noted for the effectiveness of his charms to protect livestock. One charm which he produced copiously was the talisman against enemies. Cross Smith had given clear instructions for its manufacture in his magazines: it was to be cast from tin when the planet Jupiter was in a good aspect with the sun. This, however, must only be done on the day of Jupiter and in his hour. The writing around the talisman must be done on the day and hour of Mercury, and both operations could only take place on a waxing moon. Such instructions would have made things awkward except for the most determined practitioner of the arte. If all was performed as the arte demanded and the talisman was worn in secret then the wearer was assured that they would have victory over enemies and be defended against their machinations. They would also be granted confidence and no harm would befall them.

THE LLANYBLODWEL CHARM

One final charm from the collection of the National Library of Wales is more complex and appears to have been sanctified by the use of sacrifice. This charm was found wrapped in a blood-soaked stocking that was now brown with age. It had been hidden behind a beam in a farmhouse, Gelli Bach, at Glyn Ceriog, near Llangollen. The amount of blood that is soaked into the stocking is suggestive of an animal and not simply the conjuror cutting themselves and dripping a few drops on the material. The farmhouse had been abandoned in 1880 and the charm had been created to protect the farm and its activities. While there has been some speculation about its age and providence, it is not unreasonable to assume that the charm had been created after the publication of Ebenezer Sibley's work, '*Illustration of the Occult Sciences.*'

This is because there is some material from this publication which had been used in the invocations. Sibley's work had also been used by a conjuror from Rhayader, Radnorshire, in 1850, examples of whose conjurations were produced in court which clearly showed that he was using Sibley's material for the confection of his charms.

The Glyn Ceriog charm has a six-pointed star drawn upon it with *Tetragrammaton* and *Agla* written inside. The charm has also the following wording written with it:

> '...*I who am the servant of H.L. Hughes and by the virtue*
> *of the Holy Name Immanuel sanctify unto myself*
> *the circumference of one mile around about me.*
> *X X X From the east Glanrah from the west Garran*
> *From the north Cabon from the south Berith.*
> *Which ground I take for my proper defence from*
> *all malignant spirits, witchcraft and enchantments*
> *that they may have no power over my soul or body*
> *nor come beyond these limitations*
> *nor dare to transgress their bounds.*
> *WARRA WARRA HARE IT QAMBALAN X X X...*'

The above magical formula from Sibley's work formed part of the consecration of the magical circle prior to the evocation of a spirit.

The conjuror obviously had some familiarity with Sibley's text as they had adapted it to suit their purpose. The spirit Berith, who is attributed to the south in this working, is from the '*Lesser Key of Solomon.*' While in recent times there have been several renditions of the grimoire the attribution of the Goetia spirits to the compass points is not widely known, and it is not clear in the published accounts in which directions the goetia spirits are summoned. But curiously the conjuror knew that the spirit is correctly associated with the south.

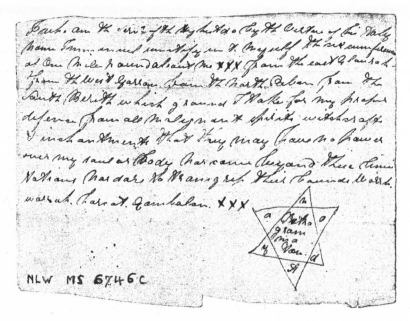

THE GLYN CERIOG CHARM

NLW MS 6746

Transcript

of undated paper.

Nantyr 15/9/30

I who am the servt of H.L.Hughes & do by the virtue of his Holy
name Immanuel sanctify unto myself the circumference of one mile
round about me XXX from the east Glanrah from the West Garran
from the North Caban from the south Berith which ground I take
for my proper defence from all maligaant spirits witchcraft &
inchantments that they may have no power over my soul or body
nor come beyond these limitations nor dare to transgress their
bounds Warrh warrah hare at Qasbalan XXX

Note:—On the partial demolition of Gelli
bach, Glyn-Ceiriog, the paper of which
the above is a transcript, was found
inside a child's stocking, made into
a long mitten, wrapped in a piece of
printed material, and placed under the main
beam of this old farm house, which has
been disused for over fifty years.

TRANSCRIPT OF THE CHARM

Dec. 4, 1930

Dear Sir,
                    Charm against Witchcraft.

         The first sentence reads - 'I who am the serv[t]
of the Highest do by the virtue of his Holy name' etc.
The word in the triangles is Tetragrammaton (Tetra /gram/ma/
ton) which means the word of four letters, and which was
used by the Hebrews to denote God, as they seldom uttered
His name; and the letters in the small triangles, when read
counter-clockwise from the bottom, form Adonay, one of the
Hebrew names of God. The other words may be Cabalistic, but
we have not seen other examples of their use, and they do
not occur in any of the other charms which are at present
in the National Library. /

         It is difficult to say when the charm was written.
The above reading does away with the question of the occupation
of the farm by a Hughes. The handwriting may well have been
of the eighteenth century, but on the other hand one would
expect to find an archaic hand on a document of a later date
in things of this nature. It is unfortunate that the paper is

LETTER CONCERNING THE CHARM

It is not often that clear identification of a past conjuror can be assumed, but with the Glyn Ceriog charm this may be possible.

This is because at Llanrhaedr Ym Mochnant, which is some twelve miles south of Glyn Ceriog, there is an unusual tombstone situated in the south-eastern corner of the churchyard that bears an inscription upon it written in the magical script known as Theban.

This magical alphabet appears in the works of both Cornelius Agrippa and Francis Barrett, but it is attributed to the magical scholarship of the 13th-century cleric Peter de Abano. Yet on this tombstone and also upon another stone at nearby Llanfyllyn, although twenty-five years apart, it is used as part of a memorial. The tombstone at Llanrhaedr is dated 1828 and is a memorial to Jane the wife of Evan Jones, of nearby Pentre. One must consider where Evan Jones acquired the Theban script. While Agrippa being the source is unlikely, but not impossible, it is more probable to have been accessed from Barrett's 1801 work '*The Magus*.' That members of the Montgomeryshire farming community could access such magical texts was owing to the actions primarily of the almanack makers, who advertised such works. And also, among others, the London booksellers Lackington and Allen, who offered one hundred and fifty occult books to the public. The almanacs were read by many, with '*Old Moore's*' selling 40,000 annually. Therefore, it is quite clear that there was a significant demand from the public for such information.

An account of a conjuror from Llanrhaedr has survived and was published in the 1873 edition of the *Montgomeryshire Collections* Vol. VI. This is an annual publication concerning the history of the county of Montgomeryshire produced by the Powysland Club. The account was written by T.W. Hancock and concerned characters of interest in and around Llanrhaedr. It dates the conjuror to 1828, which puts him in the locality at the time of the inscription on the tombstone. The conjuror and his activities are described as follows:

> '*...about forty-five years ago there lived in this parish (Llanrhaedr) a regular professional medical man who loved to wave a wand and call up spirits from the vasty deep and put them down again, and act the*

oracle in divinations. The country people called him 'bwm baili'r cythraul' (the devil's bum bailiff) Whenever he assumed to practice the black art he would wear a cap of sheepskin with a high crown, bearing a plume of pigeon's feathers, and a coat of an unusual pattern, with broad hems, and covered with talismanic characters. In his hand he held a whip, the thong of which was made of the skin of an eel and the handle of bone. With this he drew a circle around him, outside of which, at a proper distance, he kept those persons who came to him whilst he went through his mystic sentences and performances...'

One may consider how many people could this describe? Bearing in mind that Llanrhaedr has a population of about three hundred people, similar to today, it would not be unreasonable to conclude that this is a description of the originator of the Theban script that is carved on the tombstone. Indeed, as Glyn Ceriog is only a few miles to the north of Llanrhaedr, one cannot help but muse upon this, and to consider whether this conjuror was also the creator of the charm that was found at Glyn Ceriog - and whether he can therefore be named as Evan Jones.

Although he is not the only conjuror to have his dress recorded.

The celebrated cunning-woman (dynes hysbys) Hem Jem caused a sensation when she appeared at the Brecon petty sessions wearing her magical robes of purple silk.

Curiously a second tombstone at Llanfyllyn, a few miles from Llanrhaedr, also has an inscription carved upon it in Theban. This stone is dated 1856 and bears the name of Catherine Edwards, wife of David Edwards, and her daughter. Although whether there is a connection between the two families is something which is yet to be explored.

However protective charms have also been found at Llanfyllyn and are dated to the middle of the 19th-century. Again, they bear the seal from Scott's work, as with the others drawn in the bottom right-hand corner of the charm.

The Reverend T. James, the rector of Llanerfyl, Montgomeryshire, gave the following account of a charm that was found among the possessions of one of his dead parishioners:

'...*Mrs Mary Jones of Rhosgall in this parish died the other day and her executor asked me if I would help him to go through her papers. In one of her private draws I found a small round bottle about the length and thickness of my finger. It was corked and sealed.*

The cleric's account goes on to say that inside was two small rolled papers and the bottle had to be broken to get them out. One was written in Latin and the other in English:

✛ The sign of the holy Cross will defend me William Jones from present, past and future ills, both external and internal.

'Let everything that has hath breath praise the Lord.' (Ps150.v6)

'Let God arise and his enemies be scattered.' (Ps 68.v.3)

✛ Jesus ✛ Christ ✛ Messiah ✛ Emmanuel ✛ Saviour ✛ Lord of Hosts

✛ God ✛ The Everlasting (Exod. 3. 14) ✛ Jehovah ✛ The Ineffable One

✛ Agla ✛ Only Begotten ✛ Majesty ✛ The Comforter ✛ Saviour ✛ Our ✛ Mighty Lamb ✛ Adonetus ✛ Jasper ✛ Milchior ✛ Mathew ✛ Mark

✛ Luke ✛ John ✛ Amen.

The Rev. James was clearly perturbed by this discovery as he says that he was saddened to find that such beliefs in charms were still prevalent so late in the 19th century and he feared 'other practices' had also survived too.

TOMBSTONE AT LLANRHAEDR
THE THEBAN INSCRIPTION SAYS
'SACRED TO THE'

TOMBSTONE AT LLANFYLLYN

CLOSE VIEW OF THE LLANFYLLYN TOMBSTONE

CHAPTER FOUR

Of Charmers and Conjurors

'En canna I not casten the planets?'
Wizard Beguildy
Precious Bane, Mary Webb

Unlike modern witchcraft practices today, the magical activities which the local populace resorted to in times of need were of a more 'earthy' concern. Today the methods of the modern witch are by and large, but not by all, more of a religious nature than the working of magic to resolve a specific problem, and their magical operations are on the whole less malefic. For the modern witch, their craft is more concerned with religious devotion, feminist concerns and green politics. These are all good things in their own right, but they are not the witchcraft that was practised in the past. Why this emphasis has changed is another matter, perhaps it reflects the changes in society that have taken place in the last century?

There are not many trials for witchcraft in the region, and when the Witchfinder Gideon Planke in 1646 arrived in South Shropshire he was given very short shrift; being tied to a tree and killed. Planke had originally been hunting witches in East Anglia with Matthew Hopkins, who was better known as the 'Witch Finder General'. Having parted company with Hopkins, Planke thought he could create the same terror on the border and profit therefrom. The locals were having none of it and in time he became a figure in a rhyme that was used to threaten unruly children with.

Of the four trials for witchcraft in Shropshire, nobody was burnt, although Mrs Foxley of Shrewsbury was burnt alive in the Quarry for poisoning her husband. Burning could be used in matters of treason, and for a wife to poison her husband was considered at the time to be a treasonable act. However, in 1570

Bessie of Belle Vue, Shrewsbury, was found guilty of bewitching her neighbour's pig, although the sentence is not recorded.

Three other trials for witchcraft that were held in Shropshire all gave a not guilty verdict on the defendant.

1659 - Janet Wright... delivered at Shrewsbury gaol on 11th August for the suspected crime of witchcraft and murder of Amos Spenser.

1663 - Joseph Wright – delivered to Shrewsbury gaol on the 14th March for the use of incantations.

1666 – Maria Davys delivered at Shrewsbury gaol 4th August for the art of fascination.

Whether the individuals had in fact been using the occult artes is another matter, there were times when the charge would be laid to cover something else, as in the trial for witchcraft which took place at Montgomery in 1579.

David Lloid ap John of Mynod, who was described as a gentleman, brought a charge of enchantment and witchcraft against Gruffydd ap David ap John, and others. The case was heard by Sir John Throckmorton Kt, Justice of Montgomery. It was alleged that the defendants had ungodlily and diabolically conspired together. Not only by enchantments and witchcraft but by the invocation of evil spirits had enchanted an apple, delivering the same to Margaret verch David, the accuser's daughter, together with certain powder in like manner enchanted. This had the diabolical purpose of bewitching her, an undefiled virgin, to allure her to run away with Gruffydd ap John a light, lewd and evilly-disposed person and a married man with many children. Having eaten of the apple she had become immediately bewitched and had been taken away by the defendants against her will to the County of Denbighshire, where Gruffydd ap John had feloniously ravished her.

Of this case I have not been able to determine the outcome, but I would suspect it would have gone against the defendant, as no doubt the father brought the case in an attempt to salvage his daughter's reputation. At the Radnor Great Session held at Presteigne before William Foxwisted on the 30th August 1658, Owen Jones, who was described as a yeoman, was charged that on the 20th June that year he did at nearby Knighton use witchcraft pretend to give knowledge to several persons of goods lost. He was found guilty, but the sentence again is unknown.

Although most of the ecclesiastical records of the diocese of Hereford before 1700 have not survived, some accounts of the views and experiences of the border clerics make it quite clear that the services of the conjuror were widely available. Various inquiries among the parishes of the diocese which extended into parts of Radnorshire, made after the Restoration, enquired whether there were any people who resorted to charms, spells and witchcraft to heal livestock and to cure their neighbour. Yet according to one account, people still flocked to see the conjuror 'like bees to the vine.'

It was common to place rowan branches among the corn on May eve to protect the crop. Despite clerical hostility to the conjuror, who they considered to be a deceiver of mankind, there was no call for a campaign of secular punishment for them. Perhaps it was a lost cause and as such, would only create opposition to the church?

However, the local churches preferred to emphasise the responsibility of the individual for their own spiritual wellbeing and to argue that this would be impaired by associating with the conjuror, despite any perceived benefits. It was considered that the individual should accept the judgements of God and not to interfere with divine will. In times of illness the first person to be consulted should have been the priest, then a medical practitioner who was approved of by the church authorities. The conjuror should not be approached under any circumstances. Yet this was ignored and the conjuror became an important source of help for the community in times of trouble. This attitude didn't change through the passing of time.

One case that demonstrates this is recorded in the Victorian magazine 'Shreds and Patches.' In the July 1875 edition, an old man of seventy years approached an individual to write a letter on his behalf to Mrs P__ of Wellington who was a noted wise woman. He was worried that his ill wife, who was eighty, and their daughter and her two children, had been bewitched and he was now worried about his pig. He planned to pay her a shilling after his next payday if she would use her skills to protect them all. However, despite the writer of the letter trying to reason the old man out of his course of action he would not be convinced otherwise. Realising that he could not change his mind he wrote the letter on his behalf. The letter said as follows:

> '... *from the old man and his daughter at Donnington wood.*
> *The daughter's two children are ill and the old woman is ill*
> *and I want you to stop it. The old man has got a pig and he hopes*
> *you will stop anything being done to that and that one of us will see*
> *you this weekend...'*

The letter writer asked the old man what name he wanted it signed in and he replied that there was no need to sign it as the old woman would know who it was from, presumably through her powers.

It was common in many parts of the country, and in this locality too, for local women to glean the fields after harvest. This practice would often allow the poor to collect enough grain for a sack of flour if they were lucky. This could go a long way in feeding the families through the winter months, but although it was customary within the rural communities, it was often begrudged by the farmers. Writing in her book *'Shropshire Folklore,'* published in 1884, Charlotte Burne recounts how during the earlier part of the 19th century Jean Salvage, who lived near Little Drayton in North Shropshire and had a reputation as a witch, was gleaning with her neighbour in a nearby field. When the farmer came and stopped them, she cursed the man that neither man nor beast would work for him; subsequently, he found that he could get no help nor any horse to move, and the rest of his corn lay unharvested. After three days, and at his wits' end, he relented and approached the witch and allowed her to glean as much as she and her neighbour wanted without hindrance.

Another story from the same collection concerns the case of the Ambler family who farmed at Pulverbatch. Near to the farm, at Betchcott, lived an old woman called Betty Chidley. She was frequently begging at farmhouses in the area and generally was given what she asked for. One day when she called at the Ambler's farm and asked for some food, she was turned away with harsh words. At the time the farmer's wife was mixing a little meal in a pail of milk for the calves to feed. At this response, Betty Chidley remarked, *'the calves wunna et the suppin' now.'* At the time little notice was taken of her words, but the calves stopped eating. After the third day the old woman was sent for and was asked to take the spell off. *'Me bless your calves?'* she remarked. *'What have I to do with them?'* But at last she yielded to their requests and agreed to lift the spell. *'My God bless thy calves.'* She said, and still they wouldn't eat. Then the farmer's wife begged to leave out the word *'My.'* Eventually the old woman did as she was asked and said *'May God bless the calves.'* This broke the spell and soon the calves were feeding as normal.

One final account from the same collection, whereby the witch uses the word *'My God,'* is the story of Priss Morris from Cleobury North, near Ludlow. Again, a farmer resents her gleaning his fields after harvest and refuses her permission. Subsequently the farmer goes past her house with his wagon, but the horses stop at her approach and wouldn't move. Despite the farmer shouting and whipping his horses, they still would not move. Realising that the witch has cast a spell upon his horses he says to her…

> *Wad 'n thee bin doin' at my 'orses?'*
> *'I anna bin doin' nuthin.'* she remarks.
> *'Yes you 'an, see 'eres a good level road an' they canna get by thy 'ouse. Youm been doin' summat to 'em and if thee dunna tek it off I'll flog thee unto thee canna stir from the spot.'* says the farmer.
> *'I 'anna done nuthin' to 'em.'* she says again.
> *'You'm mun say pray God bless you en your 'orses, or I'll flog 'ee till thy canna stand.'*
> *'My God bless thy 'orses.'* she says at last.
> *'No, no that wunna do. I'll have nuthin' to do with thy God. You mun say may God bless thee and thy 'orses.'*

Eventually she says the words and the horses move off. The immobilising of animals and people is a magical skill that appears in the Icelandic sagas and also the Mabinogion, and it is a skill that is used among the Shropshire witches too. It is an old idea that witches have the power to stop animals and people from moving, and is one that is also apparent in various accounts of European folklore.

In the earlier years of the 19th century there lived not far from Bishop's Castle, on Todleth Hill, at nearby Churchstoke, a conjuror called Todley Tom. Although he was a farm labourer, he was noted among other things for his skill as an astrologer. He was also noted for malefic acts of magic when motivated, but was often approached to know the outcome of cockfights that took place in the area, which many of the local populace were keen on.

Burne recalls how Job Roberts, who worked for Mr Berwick at More Farm, some three miles away, visited Tom to find out whether he would be called upon to join the army to fight Napoleon. Tom takes his time coming to his conclusion and the querent becomes impatient with Tom for an answer, but is told to wait.

After he is given his answer, which Burne doesn't record, Tom asks him how he would like to travel home. 'High, low or level' are the options offered. Job chooses high as he was alarmed that he might get caught in the hedges on his way back. At Tom's word he suddenly finds himself travelling through the air and presently lands safely in the farmyard in front of his astonished friends.

Such stories of people being transported through the air are recorded among Welsh folklore with the 'Bwbach' which carries people through the air and offers them the choice of travelling above the wind, amid the wind, or below the wind.

One popular method for detecting a theft was the use of the bible and door key. This was a popular working in South Shropshire to find out the culprit. This simple working entailed that the bible should be opened at the first chapter of Ruth and while verse sixteen (Whither thou goest I will go…) was being read aloud the key should be balanced on two fingers. The key would move at the mention of the person who had committed the crime. This method was recorded at the Ludlow Borough sessions 8th January 1879, when Martha Cad was charged with the use of abusive language. The previous month she had noted that some of her washing had been removed from her garden, and with the help of a neighbour, she resorted to the Bible and key method of detection. Standing outside a nearby house, she performed the time-honoured rite, as custom demanded; but the key remained motionless. As they approached the house of Elizabeth Oliver, and mentioned her name, the key moved and the Bible jumped out of her hands. When an attempt was made to divine whether the theft had taken place at night or during the day the key declared that it had taken place during the daytime. This led Martha Cad to confront Elizabeth Oliver with the alleged crime, using a 'nice derangement of epitaphs,' that she was a daylight thief.

Elizabeth denied this and had Martha Cad charged with using abusive language. However, the whole story came out in court, which then renewed the wrangle between the pair. Several people came forward to testify that the key and bible was a true and tried method that the local people relied on to get to the truth of matters.

Although the bench dismissed the case, this was not the only time that such matters were aired before the bench. Four years later, Caroline Pardoe of Upper Gaolford, Ludlow had a watch disappear from the room in which her daughter had died. Suspecting that a neighbour had stolen the watch she 'turned the key on the Bible.' At the mention of her neighbour, Ellen Wall, the key fell to the ground and this happened when the operation was repeated. On the evidence of this divination she accused Ellen Wall of the theft, which she denied. But Wall then had her charged before the Ludlow Borough Sessions on 13th February 1883 with using abusive language. The bench was left in no doubt of what Pardoe thought of the matter as she had taken a cross summons out for the same offence against Wall's son. The bench, perhaps out of exasperation, issued a shilling fine on both parties.

However not all members of the law were such unbelievers in the occult artes. In 1861, when the police at Ludlow were having difficulty in solving a theft they used the services of the local conjuror to help with the detection of the crime. The conjuror walked the length off Corve Street, with his divining rod held before him and a large crowd gathering behind. Eventually he stopped outside a particular house, which he declared was the home of the thief and that the missing goods were in there too.

On entering the premises, the police found the goods and that the conjuror was right, much to the pleasure of the bystanders. Although the clergy of all denominations would often denounce such practices as being 'Contrary to the Word of God,' it was to no avail. When a cleric who dwelt on the Clee Hill, outside Ludlow, remonstrated with his flock against the use of charms and acts of divination, he was advised that he was wasting his time, as such practices were deeply ingrained within the local community and that this was what they did.

Probably the best example of how Shropshire, in particular, was steeped in superstition and fear of the witch, is demonstrated with the murder of Nanny Morgan on the 12th September 1857. Nanny Morgan had lived near Much Wenlock at Westwood, and in the 1880's was still remembered as a witch that no one would dare cross. Such was the awe that she was held in that at her death the mayor of Much Wenlock, William Nicolas, was obliged to have her books and possessions burnt on a bonfire in front of the Guild Hall as means to pacify the locality.

Nanny had started life as Ann Williams, which can be seen from a letter that was in possession of Charlotte Burne. Finding herself with Mary Beamond being held in Shrewsbury prison, with both women being held on a charge of theft from Mrs Powell of Bourton, near Much Wenlock, Nanny had written the following letter to her parents.

Salop prison March 16th 1809
This comes with my dutey to you and my Mother, and I hope you will send me sum money as I have imploied Atturney and a counsellor and I hope I shall see you up a Long with Me as the time his draing very near at hand as the Asizes begin tomorrow week and I think you had better com up the day before and Mary Beamond bids to be remembered to hur Mother and hur geet hur sum money for hur with out fail and send it or bring it with hur wen hur coms a long with you. Pleas to send us an answer to hus as soon as Possible you can so no more at present.
From your dutiful dauter Ann Williams
Mary Beammun

At the trial Mary Beamond was found guilty of the charge and Nanny was freed; on leaving Shrewsbury, she took up with some gypsies from whom she learnt the artes of conjure and divination. After a wandering life she eventually settled in her home area at Westwood Common between Much Wenlock and Bourton. Living here she soon built up a fearsome reputation as an accurate diviner and people from all walks of life consulted her. So much so that at her death several letters were found from prominent people concerning work that she had done for them. Also present was a quantity of jewellery assumed to be in payment for her services from those who had surreptitiously made use of her services. It was said of Nanny that she was consulted by servant girls from miles around and by people who should have known better.

> '…everyone were frightened of her.' say the Wenlock folk and no one durst say refuse her nothing for fear she should do something at them. And she kep' a box of live toads in the house and the place fair swarmed with cats.'

So Burne's account tells us.

But in the September 1857, she was murdered by her lodger William Davies who was half her age. Nanny and Davies had lived together in a cottage on the side of the road from Wenlock to Church Stretton.

However, the reporting of the trial at Shrewsbury, and published in the Shrewsbury Chronicle make it quite clear from the accounts of various witnesses that the community was in fear of her and her magical abilities. The evidence given by Ann Jane Edwards, as recorded by the press at the time, testifies to this.

> '…I have known the deceased ever since I was a child.
> She was a strong and powerful woman…
> She had the reputation as being a fortune teller.
> The people in the neighbourhood were afraid of her.
> She was supposed to be a person of great power.
> She was reported to possess that power known as the evil eye
> and was consulted upon the loss of goods and the ailments of cattle.
> I have been told that she professed to cast nativities
> and tell fortunes.'

She also says the following about William Davies…

> '…*He told me that it was as if she had bewitched him – the power she had over him. He has told me she possessed some very bad books – books of witchcraft and magic. She said she would not let him look at them and that if he were to look at them when she was out, he would raise the devil. He told me this seriously. It seemed to me that she had possessed him with the notion of her powers of witchcraft and magic and that she could draw him into the magic circle. He said that she had told him that spirits talked to her.*
> *….She was a person much dreaded and feared by almost all persons in the neighbourhood, in consequence of these fancied powers.'*

On the cross-examination of Robert Birkin, a neighbour, he makes it quite clear that…

> '…*She had a very bad character in the neighbourhood;*
> *and was reputed to be a witch.*
> *It was generally supposed that she could tell fortunes*
> *and influence the fate of people.*
> *If anything happened to a man's pig or cow*
> *her 'evil eye' was suspected.*
> *….I have heard him say that she could fetch him out of a field*
> *by some supernatural power.'*

Curiously the judge bowed to local opinion and directed the jury that if they thought that William Davies was the victim of witchcraft and that the killing of Nanny Morgan was the result thereof, then it wasn't to be considered as murder. Although he was found not guilty of murder, he received a sentence of twelve years transportation. Legend has it that the ship sunk at sea, and William Davies was drowned; it was deemed by the local populace to be the work of Nanny Morgan. That the mayor was obliged to burn her books in public as a means to pacify the locality suggests not only how deeply rooted such beliefs were among the rural populace of south Shropshire, but also the fear that it generated. It also asks the question about Nanny's books. Having in her possession magical books demonstrates how far such publications could percolate throughout all strata of society. Here, in a rural backwater, is an old woman with occult books, and the ability to cast an astrological chart, and to give a judgement based upon the movement of the stars. Thus in 19th-century rural Shropshire was an elderly woman who was studying and working with an occult science that would have been recognised in ancient Babylon where so many of the rules of astrology were devised.

And of course, books cost money. One hundred and fifty years ago they would have been only for the most seriously committed practitioner and not for those for whom it was a whim or a passing fancy, the cost in such times of want would be prohibitive for many of the rural poor which says something about Nanny Morgan's interest.

CHAPTER FIVE

Dyn Hysbyn

'I charge all witches and ghosts
to depart from this house.
In the Great Name of Jehovah and Alpha and Omega.'
A charm found at Madeley, 1882

Two conjurors of note are John Harries (1785-1839) and his son Henry (1821-49), of Cwrt y Cadno, Caeo, near Llandovery.

Although they are on the periphery of the area under consideration, I include them as so many people from Mid Wales would consult with them in times of need. The elder Harries had, when young, received sufficient education to become a surgeon and to develop a practice in Harley Street London. At this time he became good friends with Robert Cross Smith. Writing in 1904 of the '*History of Caio,*' F.S. Price of Swansea records how popular the Harries were in the area.

He remarked how....

The sick and the sorrowful came from all parts of Wales and they were eminently successful in their cures.

Lunatics were brought to them from parts of Pembrokeshire and Radnorshire and they had a wonderful power of them.

The course of treatment would include what he would term his water treatment, and the bleeding treatment. One of his chief methods was, he would take the afflicted to the brink of the river and fire an old flint revolver, this would frighten the patient to such a degree that he would fall into the pool.

He assumed the power of charming away pain, and was so successful that people believed thoroughly that he was in league with the evil one.'

Owen Davies, writing in his work *'Cunning-folk in English History,'* gives an account of a man from Radnorshire who went to see the Harries for a cure of his stammer. They stood him by a deep bend in the river and fired the gun over his head. This startled him so much that he fell in the cold water with the resultant shock thereof curing him!

While the Harries were noted healers with their use of charms, herbs and shock therapy, they were often approached for help in finding lost objects or people. They were also contacted for help with exorcism of people and places.

One example of the former concerned a man who had become convinced that he had become bewitched. Several doctors had been approached for help, with little being forthcoming. When the family asked the Harries for help, at first they were rebuked for not coming earlier and wasting time with 'quacks and charlatans' who could offer nothing in such cases. The family were told that the man had swallowed an evil spirit in the form of a tadpole, which had now grown into a frog. After making a show of consulting their books and paraphernalia they induced the man to vomit and lo - in the vomit was a frog and the man was cured!

The Harries were often consulted about the future and what it held for their clients. Henry Harries issued the following proclamation, describing his work as a dyn hysbyn. He suggested that he could determine....

> *'...temper, disposition, fortunate or unfortunate in their general pursuits, honour, riches, journeys and voyages (success therein and what places best to travel to or reside in)*
> *friends and enemies, trade or profession best to follow and whether fortunate in speculation etc. Of marriage if to marry. The description, temper, disposition of the person, rich or poor, happy or unhappy in marriage.*
> *Of children whether fortunate or not, deduced from the sun and moon, with planetary orbs at the time of their birth.*
> *Also of disease and sickness.'*

In the collections of the National Library of Wales are various books and items of interest that had once belonged to the Harries, which give an idea of their practice and relationships with the local people. There are several of their astrological charts which they had drawn up for their clients. These charts are square in nature, similar to the charts used by medieval astrologers instead of the modern round pattern which is now used. There are two conjurations of interest and a template for unpaid bills for services rendered that can be individually completed for specific clients. Also in the collection is a grimoire with which they worked. This grimoire is based upon sixty-five of the usual seventy-two spirits of the Lesser Key of Solomon, also known as the Goetia. The eminent grimoire scholar David Rankine suggests that the likely source for the Harries' grimoire confection would have been garnered from French sources as there were variants of this grimoire based upon sixty-five spirits and not the full seventy-two being used within French occult circles. Their grimoire also included spirits from the little-known work *Theurgia-Goetia*.

It is quite clear that they had access to the corpus of the Western Magical Traditions, and if they did, then no doubt other conjurors had too; probably all drawing upon the same resources for their workings. One account of their magical sources was explicitly given by J.C. Davies who had visited the Harries and had gained access to their books. He wrote down the details of an invocation which they used, which is taken from Scott's work, although it also appears in the *Pauline Art of King Solomon*:

> '...*after this is done let him compose a prayer unto the said Genius, which must be repeated thrice every morning for seven days before the invocation..... When the day had come when the magician would invoke his prayer to the Genius he must enter into a private closet, having a little table and silk carpet, and two waxen candles lighted; and a crystal stone shaped about the quantity of an apple. The stone must be fixed upon a frame in the centre of the table; and then, proceeding with great devotion to invocate, he must thrice repeat the former prayer concluding the same with Pater Noster etc, and a missale de Spiritu Sancto.*
> *Next he must consecrate the candles, carpet, table and crystal, sprinkling the same with his blood and saying:*

I do by the power of the Holy Names
Aaglon, Eloi, Eloi, Sabbath, On, Aneoturaton, Jah, Again, Jah,
Jehovah, Immanuel, Archon, Archonton, Sadai, Adai etc...
sanctifie and consecrate these holy utensils to the performance of this
holy work. In the name of the Father, Son and Holy Ghost Amen.
When done, the exorcist must say the following prayer with his face
towards the east and kneeling with his back to the consecrated table
saying....
O blessed Phanael, my angel guardian
vouchsafe to descend with thy holy influence
and presence into this spotless crystal
that I may behold thy glory.
This prayer being first repeated towards the east, must afterwards be
said towards all the four winds thrice... And next the 70th psalm
repeated out of a bible that hath been consecrated in the manner as
the rest of the utensils, which ceremonies being performed, the
magician must arise from his knees and sit before the crystal
bareheaded with the consecrated bible in his hand and the waxen
candle new lighted waiting patiently and intently for the coming of and
appearance of the Genius. Now about a quarter of an hour before the
spirit come, there will appear a great variety of apparitions within the
glass, at first a beaten road or track with travellers, men and women
marching silently along. Next there will appear rivers, wells,
mountains. After that a shepherd upon a hill feeding a goodly flock
of sheep and the sun shining brightly at his going down, and lastly
innumerable flows of birds and beasts, monsters and strange
appearance and which will all vanish at the appearance of the
Genius.'

Yet again as with Nanny Morgan, in a rural backwater occult practices were being undertaken with a magical formula that has changed little since its use in the Greco-Egyptian world; and perhaps even further back.

In the collections at Aberystwyth, the Harries have left various medical accounts and receipts for medicines, prescriptions, lectures and a treatise on urine. However, the failure to pay for any medicines would quickly be followed by a printed statement....

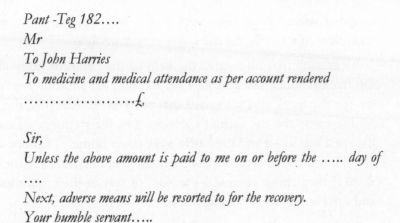

Pant -Teg 182....
Mr
To John Harries
To medicine and medical attendance as per account rendered
......................£

Sir,
Unless the above amount is paid to me on or before the ..... day of
....
Next, adverse means will be resorted to for the recovery.
Your humble servant.....

Although the Harries often assisted in the search for missing people or property, this was not without hazard. When John Harries assisted with the search for a missing girl, by the use of his arte, and described the location where she would be found, he quickly found himself apprehended as an accessory to her murder. He duly appeared before two magistrates at Llandovery, Lwyd Glansefin and Gwyn Glanbran. When Harries offered to demonstrate his skills to the two magistrates as part of his defence, he suggested that if they told him the time when they came into the world, he would tell them the time when they would leave. Both magistrates declined and released Harries from the charges against him.

On one occasion a farmer approached them for help in finding his cattle which had been either lost or stolen. They told him to come back the next day when they would have the information for him that he required. The farmer agreed as he had come some way for their help, but with the hour being late, unknown to the Harries the farmer took shelter for the night in a nearby barn.

Early in the morning Harries senior arrived in the barn and proceeded to draw his circle of arte on the floor to conjure the spirits.

Eventually, he was told where the cows would be the following noon, the farmer hearing this crept off without saying anything to either of the Harries. Finding his cattle as predicted he rounded them up to take back home but they wouldn't move: regardless of what he did the cows were immobile.

Realizing that he needed the help of the conjuror he returned. On his arrival he was rebuked for running off without paying the fee for the Yr work and informed that the Harries had placed a spell on the cattle for the farmer's slyness. On the payment of the fee the spell was lifted and the cattle were taken home. That conjurors could know the movements of their enemies and inflict harm upon them if they chose created a measure of fear in their communities and the Harries were no exception.

One example given by Maria Trevelyan demonstrated this ability to inflict punishment where they felt it was justified. On one occasion when they were visiting, with others, the home of a prominent individual, the Harries were admiring the garden with their host. When they asked if they could sample some fruit from a nearby tree they were denied. At this Harries encouraged the man to get his ladder and climb up the tree to inspect the fruit at the top. Climbing up the tree the man suddenly found that he was immobilised and couldn't get down. Harries left him up the tree for the rest of the afternoon as a lesson in good manners.

Because both Harries were noted conjurors who could often find lost objects with their arte, there were times that if something went missing the owner only had to mention that they were going to consult with the conjuror and the missing item would return.

Writing in *The Red Dragon* (1886) Helen Watney remarked how her mother had once cause to suspect that one of her servants had stolen a set of silver spoons. By mentioning that she would shortly be consulting with the Harries the spoons re-appeared in a short time.

Both Harries were respected astrologers and had a client base from far and near. Having issued an advertising card with the heading 'Nativities Calculated,' the Harries were satirised in the journal 'Yr Haul,' but instead of creating adverse publicity for the Harries' astrological practice it produced the opposite effect and increased their client base over a much wider area. The questions that they were asked ranged over all human concern. Thomas Thomas of Pen-lon asks 'If a certain person will be their wife.'

Another William Powell asks about the return of some missing cattle (the answer to be left at the Swan Inn). A third example concerns William Lloyd who wrote to the Harries on behalf of his sister regarding the pain in her breast; the chart for this still exists at Aberystwyth, with the following letter.

> *Dear Sir,*
> *My sister desire you to do your best you can for them. Mary Ann have a pain in the breast will you please send (unreadable)*
> *Mary Ann Lloyd was born May 21ˢᵗ 1823, it was on a Sunday at four o'clock in the morning.*

Although details of the treatment which they advised is not recorded the chart below gives us a glimpse into the situation.

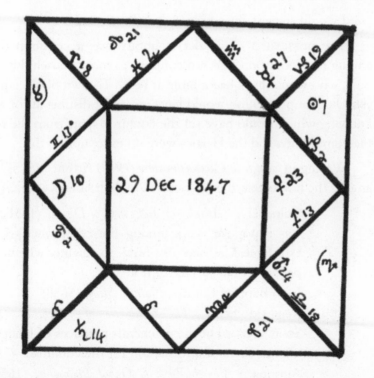

This is a medieval square chart, a style the Harries were familiar with.

This would be known as a decumbiture chart, that is a chart cast when the astrologer is asked about an illness, it'll be for the moment they open the letter and read about the case. Luna is in the first house which is good and as the chart is about a female this shows that the chart is fit to judge. The sixth house is ruled by Libra which is fitting for the female breast. However Mars is domiciled therein, and this is not good.

But Mars is weak in Libra and as its sign Scorpio is incapacitated this will weaken the power of Mars. It could suggest an inflammation, perhaps an abscess? Venus, the planet who rules Libra, is in the seventh house and favoured because she is angular and in the house Sagittarius, which is favourable.

The medicine is ruled by the tenth house which is Aquarius, suggesting a cooling medicine, which would have traditionally been prescribed for a hot condition.

I would suggest she survived and all was well.

The possession of an occult library was a common feature among the conjurors. This ran contrary to most households of the time, who would have had a bible at best. To own books among a semi-literate population would have created a distinct air of arcane knowing which would have set the conjuror apart from the rest of the community; and the Harries were no exception to this.

Writing in '*Magic in Carmarthenshire (1913)* Arthur Mee says that among the books that the Harries had in their library were....

- Culpeper... *Astrological Judgement of Disease* (1651). This was a popular work among the conjurors as it gave astrological advice on how to divine whether the patient would survive or not.
- John Baptista Porta... *Natural Magic* (1658)
- Reginald Scott...*The Discoverie of Witchcraft* (1584). Scott's record of the witchcraft practices of Kent was a major source of information for the conjuror.
- Agrippa... *Fourth Book of Occult Philosophy* (1650). A work based upon the Heptameron grimoire with sound advice on the occult for the student thereof.
- *Synopsis Medicinae* (1671). A useful compendium of medical self help.

- Also listed are several works on astrology and two astrological magazines, which also contain useful magical information.
- *The Straggling Astrologer* (1824

PANT COY
THE HARRIES' HOME AT CWRT Y CADNO

- *The Astrologer's Magazine* (1793). Also known as the Conjuror's Magazine…. Popular at the time for its horoscopes and general occult content.
- *The Complete Illustration of the Celestial Science of Astrology* (1788). This complete work by Ebenezer Sibley ran to more than a thousand pages. It was a heady mixture of astrology, divination and magic. By 1812, owing to its popularity, it had been reprinted eleven times. Although not an original work, as it drew heavily upon the works of the 17th astrologers Gadbury and William Lilly, who were often at logger-heads, nonetheless Sibley made their works and others much more

accessible to those who were endeavouring to study the occult artes.

JOHN HARRIES

Once a year the Harries would construct a magical circle in the woods and read from their book of conjuration, a volume which they always kept locked. They would take with them four others who helped them with the practice of the arte. The locals always referred to this day as the day they bargained their souls with the devil. Although what happened with the others who assisted them is not explained.

The library of the Harries was broken up in 1849 with the death of Henry Harries from consumption; the elder Harries having already died in 1839 aged 55.

Whilst other members of the family were consulted on lost items and could predict the future, none became as popular as John Harries and his son Henry.

CHAPTER SIX

Cursed Thou Be

'...You who sow discord, where are you?
You who infuse hate and propagate enmities
I direct, conjure and constrain you...'
- Mastering Witchcraft, Paul Huson

In the early 16th century William Tyndale observed how, in the March of Wales, it was a widespread custom to approach the priest to curse the thief; particularly if livestock had been stolen. They would also approach others in the community to invoke 'God's curse upon the perpetrator of the crime.' After the Reformation this approach changed, and the priest was no longer approached for help by the victim.

There were some curses that were considered to be highly effective. The curse uttered by a person upon their death bed for instance, or the curse uttered by a parent on their child, as the cursing of John Lloyd ap Richard by his mother, who fell upon her knees invoking God's wrath upon her son. The Star Chamber records how in 1612 twenty poor men were invited to sit at a feast and afterwards they knelt down with raised hands and called God's wrath down upon the heads of their host's enemies.

While there are several accounts of ritualised cursing from Herefordshire and Shropshire recorded in the ecclesiastical courts, it is clear that the cursers usually had Welsh names. In 1617 a churchwarden from Hereford complained how Joanna Powell had cursed him in the Welsh language, stating that she had knelt down on her bare knees and raised her arms to the heavens and invoked God.

The act of public cursing was a petitionary prayer to God, delivered by those who felt that they had been wronged and had no legal redress. The malediction was delivered from a kneeling position with the hands being raised up to heaven. Sometimes women would intensify the curse by laying bare their breasts while they called for the destruction of those who they were cursing, their property and persons. The invoking of fire was often a part of the curse, as can be seen when in 1681 Elizabeth Parry fell to her knees, invoking God to send down 'wild fire' from heaven to the house of Elizabeth ferch Richard. While Lucy Richards, from Welshpool, was known as a 'common curser of her neighbours.' She prayed that Jeffery Lloyd's house might burn over his head and that Lewis Reynolds would hang. And that those who helped them would not prosper, and that they might too, be an example to the whole world.

In 1684 Jane Lloyd of Llanynys, who was in a dispute over property, spoke the following curse in Welsh:

> '...melltith Duw ir neb a ddelo I'm tu i om anfodd.'
> (the curse of God on anyone who comes into my house against my will)
> She went on to pray that her enemies would never prosper...
> '...Na caffo byth gam rhwdd na byth rhwydeb
> nag iechyd a gymero nhu i.'
> (He who takes my house shall never have an easy step, prosperity, nor good health)

Yet cursing among the populace was not always aimed at the curser's neighbour, and there were times when the high and mighty of the land were also cursed. The 17th-century recording by Lord Herbert of Chirbury of how his ancestors, the Earl of Pembroke and his brother, were cursed is of note. Having been instructed by Edward IV to bring order to parts of North Wales, they approached their work with some ruthlessness, and at one point in their campaign captured seven brothers who were known felons and outlaws. The Herberts hanged them all despite the mother's plea that at least one of them be let live. The mother, armed with her rosary, knelt before them and cursed Pembroke and his brother that God's mischief might fall upon them. The following battle of Edgecote saw their demise.

Another act of cursing was invoking the powers of the Cursing Well. One thinks of a well as being benign, indeed even a place of healing, but some Welsh holy wells have a dual nature.

There are certain wells which are considered to have malefic properties as well as healing. It was believed that a local saint had in the past blessed the well accordingly and their prayers had granted this power. The well Ffynnon y Pechod, in Clywd, despite being a noted Christian well also had the power to grant the individual the ability to master the 'Dark Artes.' And a nearby well, St George's, also shared a dual nature. This well would not only cure man and beast of a wide variety of ailments but would also curse one's enemies.

Yet for many people in the locality wells that brought forth damnation and misadventure were often resorted to in times of trouble. The most famous Cursing Well in Wales was Ffynnon Elian, a well whose notorious powers were spread not only throughout Wales but further afield and which was even known of in faraway India. One practice from this well was to skewer a live frog and throw the unfortunate beast into the well; while it lived your enemy would be in torment. At other times a wax poppet representing the person to be afflicted was thrown in with curses being recited. Passages from the Bible were read out, and a cup of water was partly drunk, with the remains being thrown over one's shoulder with the uttering of the curse; this was to be done three times. It was considered that the person who was cursed would receive misfortune at every full moon.

To lift the curse, the object would have to be retrieved and certain psalms recited for the next three successive Friday nights.

Originally the well had been a healing well but its powers had been 'turned.' Despite local magistrates trying to stop people from using the well, their endeavours were unsuccessful, and the power of the well was still being invoked towards the end of the 19th-century. It was common for people in Mid Wales not only to threaten their adversaries with 'being put in the well,' but they were also known to travel to the well to fetch the waters back for cursing.

One Breconshire farmer carried two barrels back to his farm in southern Powys, where he dealt with his neighbours accordingly!

Traditionally the keeper of the well would charge them a fee, and they would write the name of the person being cursed on a piece of slate and place it in the well. While their name was in the waters bad luck would invariably be their fate, or so it was thought. Although for another fee they could be persuaded to take the name out of the well and release the person from the curse.

In 1862 a farmer from Trefeglwys, near Llanidloes, would not leave his farm as a neighbour had fetched a barrel of the waters to sprinkle around the boundaries of the man's farm. The old man hadn't left his property for twenty years, and only did so after the neighbour had died in 1882; such was the reputation of the power of the waters.

However, it was not only ordinary people who were subject to the power of the well, as shown by one 19th century non-conformist minister, who fell out with of one of his congregation and was cursed with the power of the well. Subsequently, he took to his bed and died. In the 1890's the vicar of St Asaph claimed that he knew of an individual who was owed £80 and dared not make a fuss as he had been threatened with his name being placed in the cursing well. One woman who had had enough of her husband's maltreatment made a wax poppet and pushed a pin into the head. After uttering her curse, she placed it in the well, and for months he suffered from headaches and various discomforts. Eventually he realised what she had done, after repenting his ways and mending his manners she removed the poppet from the well and lifted the curse from him.

The act of invoking the power of water to curse an opponent is not only restricted to 19th-century Mid Wales. In many respects, we can see this tradition being descended from the Celt. By considering the Roman baths at Bath, we can see how liberal the Celts had been with their curses. Archaeologists and others have found in the waters many lead curse tablets that have the victims' names inscribed upon them, and their transgressions too. In many respects, the practice of placing the victim's name in the well is quite clearly a continuation of this earlier practice.

CHAPTER SEVEN

The Sin-Eater

*'.... he shall present the live goat; and Aaron shall lay both his
hands upon the head of the live goat, and confess over him all the
iniquities of the people of Israel, and all their transgressions, all their
sins; and he shall put them upon the head of the goat, and shall send
him away into the wilderness by the hand of man who is in readiness.
The goat shall bear all their iniquities upon him to a solitary land;
and he shall let the goat go in the wilderness.'*
- *Leviticus 16:20-22*

The Sin-eater is a figure peculiar to the Welsh border country
and some parts of Wales. One appears in the Shropshire novels of
Mary Webb, particularly 'Precious Bane,' in which Gideon eats the
sin of his father. Primarily the sin-eaters were male and were by
and large ostracized by the communities in which they lived.
When a person died the services of the sin-eater were called upon
by the family of the deceased to aid the spirit of the person in their
passing. By consuming food and drink, and also accepting a coin,
the sin of the dead person was taken on by the sin-eater.

Writing in *'Herefordshire Folklore'* Ella Leather remarks how....

*'...In the county of Hereford was an old custom at funerals to hire a
person who were to take upon them all the sins of the party deceased.
One of them I remember lived in a cottage on the Ross highway. He
was a long, lean, lamentable rascal.*
*The manner was that when the corpse was brought out of the house
and laid on the bier, a loaf of bread was given to the sin-eater over the
body, as also a bowl of beer which he drank and sixpence in money,
in consideration whereof he took upon him all the sins of the defunct
and freed them from walking after they were dead.'*

The last known sin-eater along the border was Richard Munslow who died in 1906. He lived in the Bishops Castle area of south-west Shropshire; in the locality there are still relatives of his today.

His monument was recently repaired at Ratlinghope (Ratchet to the locals) church.

As part of the ritual he would say....

> *'...I give easement and rest now to thee dear man.*
> *Come not down the lanes or in our meadows.*
> *And for thy peace I pawn my own soul. Amen'*

THE SIN-EATER'S MONUMENT, RATLINGHOPE

The sin-eater was usually a poor person, but Richard Munslow was a respected member of the farming community who farmed seventy acres at Upper Darnford. He employed three labourers and had grazing rights on the nearby Long Mynd - in many respects he was a farmer of some substance. The monument erected in the churchyard at Ratlinghope attracted widespread publicity when an appeal was launched to repair it.

CHAPTER EIGHT

Last Of The Cunning Folk?

'wunna a reg'lar doctor like, and hadna bin through no colleges,
But he can still rule the planets.'
Unknown Clun woman commenting on a local conjuror, 1881
- *Shropshire Folklore, Charlotte Burne*

The last of the Cunning Folk to find themselves before the courts was Ellen Hayward from Cinderford in the Forest of Dean. She appeared at the petty sessions in 1906 and was charged with the crime of using her skills to 'pretend witchcraft' as a means to deceive and impose upon one of His Majesty's subjects. The individual concerned was James Davies, who was a sixty-six year old hurdle maker from Worcestershire. After two of his cows and three of his pigs had become ill, a travelling woman had told him that they had been bewitched out of spite by another woman. His sister wrote to Ellen Hayward about her brother's plight and paid her 2s/6d for help.

After he had walked the thirty miles to her abode and paid her 5/- she told him what to do to protect his remaining livestock. Having followed her instructions there was an improvement for a while, but then the animals relapsed, and Davies himself became ill. Despite his ill health, he travelled to see Hayward for a third time, and asked her again for help. This time he gave her a sovereign and she told him he had flu. However, things became worse and Davies blamed Hayward for his problems, saying that she had cursed him. With this in mind, he told her that he was going to the police to complain, which alarmed her as she had already had been in trouble with the authorities over the John Markey affair.

The previous year she had been approached by John Markey to help him retrieve fifty pounds which had been stolen from him. On his insistence, she had conjured the face of the thief in a crystal and Markey realised that it was a member of his own family. This became the last straw for the Markey family, who, it would appear, were already suffering extreme signs of mental deficiency, so much so that two of the family had been incarcerated in the local Gloucester asylum. Now the neighbourhood experienced a 'witchcraft panic,' generated by the Markey family.

Not only did the rising fears reach the national papers, but they were also mentioned in the House of Commons by McVeagh M.P., the member for Down South. The adverse publicity and attention of the authorities had made Hayward wary of another repetition of her past experiences. When Davies offered her a further 2/6d for help she refused and said that God would lift the spell in his own good time. Davies then went to the police to complain. When questioned by the police she said that...

> '...I tell them what to do and they pay me for my advice.
> I have given advice on the treatment of cows, horses and pigs, but I am cautious of giving advice since the Markey affair.
> My profession is an herbalist, I am seventy years old and have done no harm to anyone.'

When she was summoned to appear before the local magistrates, she explained that she placed her faith in God who....

> 'had always promised his children should not want.'

She claimed that the only medicine she had given Davies was a simple cup of tea. She claimed that she had many satisfied customers, a claim which was supported by numerous letters sent to the court stating that she was an excellent herbalist and healer. The court dismissed the case against her. Shortly after her trial a letter appeared in the local press and was signed 'anti-oppression'. It contained the following....

> '...Sir, is there no way in the interests of the community and our boasted civilisation and good name, of putting a stop to the persecution of Mrs Hayward? Everyone locally knows the preposterous suggestion of witchcraft has no grounds. In fact, certainly the local magistrates and the police know, I think....'

The letter went on to suggest that the medical profession were interested in seeing her persecuted, as they saw her as a rival.

The letter writer also claimed that there were plenty of people in the locality who had benefited from her skills and that they should be more vocal in their support of her.

Writing in *'The Folklore of Radnorshire,'* Roy Palmer narrates the story of a police inspector at Llandrindod Wells who described in 1965 how a man reported a theft of certain property to the police. He suggested that the thief was a well-known character, much feared in the area for his occult powers. He was considered, by many people, to be a conjuror who would ill wish a person should he choose to do so. He was interviewed by the police who took no further steps in the matter. Shortly afterwards the complainant became ill and never worked again. For the rest of their life, until they died, they were plagued by ill-health and bad luck. At one point they told the inspector that they wished that they had never gone to the police over the matter as the conjuror's curse had made things worse. Palmer remarks how until very recently the conjuror and their powers were a potent force within the local communities.

CHAPTER NINE

Dramatis Personae

For Our Name is Legion
- Luke 8:30

It is a curious observation how many people of an occult persuasion have found their way to the borderlands of Wales, and this is not a modern phenomenon. In the early days of the reign of Edward IV, while he was domiciled at Ludlow Castle, he was instructed in esoteric matters by George Ripley, the alchemical Canon of Bridlington. The noted Mary Herbert, related to the Earls of Pembroke, also held an alchemical inquiry at Ludlow Castle; aided by the brother of Sir Walter Raleigh, Adrian Gilchrist. The Elizabethan era saw a small but vibrant occult community on the Welsh border with John Gwynne, mayor of Llanidloes, writing to Dr John Dee and Sir Edward Kelley regarding magical instruction and arranging for alchemical manuscripts to be translated.

One observation I have made of the modern-day occult community is that it has become dominated in its magical practice by the activities of the Victorian magical order the Hermetic Order of the Golden Dawn, and its derivatives. Something which perhaps is not as appreciated as it could be is that there was a vibrant magical current in Britain before the birth of the Hermetic Order of the Golden Dawn in 1888; aspects of which were flourishing in Shropshire.

Writing in *'Herefordshire Folklore,'* Ella Leather includes an account of Sir Edward Harley, of Brampton Bryan, Herefordshire, and his 'Berill' or shewstone. This he used for magical workings during the 1640's. She tells us that it originally came from Norfolk and where it had been in the keeping of a clergyman. She also says that it was about an inch in diameter and set in a ring of silver, with a stem about ten inches high. At the four quarters were the names of the archangels, Gabriel, Uriel, Raphael and Michael. The Harleys of Brampton Bryan are still in residence, where their illustrious ancestor, Brilliana, kept the royalist hoards at bay by blowing up their powder store in the middle of the night when they had laid siege to her home. Frederick Hockley (1808-85), who was a Victorian occultist and who left over twelve hundred accounts of his magical workings, would often visit the Harleys for magical discourse.

He was also on good terms with Walter Moseley, of Buildwas Hall near Ironbridge, Shropshire, although he says Moseley was in rather a bad ordure, as he would often use drugs and sex in his magical rituals. Hockley would also correspond with Robert Owen, founder of the Co-operative movement, who would often write to Hockley for advice and help with his own occult experimentation. Regarding this, various letters have survived between Hockley and Robert Owen, and some time ago I asked the curator at the Robert Owen Museum, at Newtown in Mid Wales, about these letters, and whether I could see them. I was politely rebuffed.

Although Hockley wasn't associated with Shropshire as such, he was a visitor who was a major influence on the magical practices of some of its people. Being a member of the Victorian magical group *The Society of Eight* and also the *Societas Rosicruciana in Anglia* (SIRA), Hockley no doubt had access to various occult works and individuals. These would surely have been influential upon his magical works and the knowledge that he passed on to others.

As would the works of Paschal Beverly Randolph, a mixed-race American, who taught the use of belladonna and hashish within ritual.

Writing in his work 'The Brotherhood of the Rosy Cross,' A.E. Waite considered that Moseley had died through his use of such drugs, which he had been encouraged to use through his association with Randolph. Whether such practices had any bearing on his death is another manner. As Randolph also taught the use of sexual energies within magical rites, and since he was on favourable terms with Moseley, this was probably Moseley's source for the information he was using within his magical practice which Hockley refers to. When Moseley died in 1885 his occult library was sold by the London publisher George Redway, and the sale took two days to complete.

Randolph was also on friendly terms with the Reverend William Ayton (1816-1909) who had spent some time at Ketley, Shropshire, where he had administered to the parish. Ayton was highly thought of by his fellow occultists such as Kenneth Mackenzie who was instrumental in promoting occult groups and was friendly with the French magus Eliphas Levi. Ellic Howe, writing in '*The Magicians of the Golden Dawn,*' says that Mackenzie considered Ayton to be a 'profound occultist.' Ayton was also on good terms with Moseley who lived nearby.

While Ayton had been a member of the '*Hermetic Brotherhood of Luxor,*' it is not clear that Moseley had been involved. The Reverend Ayton also had a profound and active interest in the alchemical arte and often worried that his bishop would find out that he had an alchemical laboratory in the cellars of his vicarage. Ayton, with his wife Anne, was among the first members of the Hermetic Order of the Golden Dawn.

They would also have known Anna Bonus Kingsford whose husband, her cousin, was the vicar at Atcham near Shrewsbury, a few miles away from Ayton's Ketley parish. The Aytons were, in turn, a few miles from Walter Moseley at Buildwas, near Ironbridge, and they would have known many of his occult contacts as well.

Anna, the vicar's wife from Atcham, who is rarely acknowledged, either for her occult influences or for her input into promoting both animal and women's rights, had in fact been highly influential upon Wescott and Mathers, the two founders of the Hermetic Order of the Golden Dawn in 1888.

Having married her cousin, she made it quite clear that she was her own woman and was not going to be just 'the vicar's wife.' Having been refused admittance to medical school in the UK, she left to study medicine in France, where she was appalled at the suffering of animals in medical research; something which she campaigned ardently against. During her time in Paris, she became part of the occult circle that gathered around Maria Pomar, Lady Caithness (1830-95), who was prominent in the theosophist movement. She claimed that Mary Queen of Scots had appeared to her and instructed her to promote a new religious current that would help reconcile the sexes at a spiritual level; she also complained about the unfairness of Mary's beheading.

Lady Caithness had offered Anna Kingsford the use of her Parisian mansion while she was in Paris, from where she promoted her campaigns supporting vegetarianism. During those heady days, she became more influenced by the occult current Lady Caithness promoted, one heavily influenced by Gnostic, Neoplatonist and Hermetic thought. And on her return to London, after qualifying and setting up her medical practice, she became involved with William Westcott and Samuel Mathers, the founders of the Hermetic Order of the Golden Dawn. Anna Kingsford's ideas on the equality of the sexes and the end of an all-male priesthood was an idea that both Westcott and Mathers agreed with, and one that was soon apparent within the magical order which they created. For her, God was both female and male, and as such it was absurd to consider that God could be anything else. She declared that, '*the perfect way was now open to women, opposed to the bestiality of men with the power of the feminine spirit.*' Subsequently she published her work *The Perfect Way*, where she favoured an esoteric Christianity which suggested that Jesus was not divine and that original sin was not true. She also declared that she was Catholic to avoid going to her husband's Church of England services, that is when she went back home.

During her sojourn in Paris, she would join the spiritual salon hosted by Lady Caithness, which such Parisian occult luminaries as Guatia, Papus, and Wirth would attend. As would Doinel, founder of the Gnostic Church and Abbe Alta who was a founder member of Guaita and Peladan's Kabbalistic Order Rose-Croix. At one session everyone became aware of the manifestation of Cathar bishops, who after sanctifying Doniel instructed him in the creation of the Gnostic church.

It was among such company that Anna Kingsford flourished, company which was a far cry from the rural backwater of her husband's parish in Shropshire. Indeed, during her time in Paris, and with the use of her occult knowledge, she started a magical campaign against the doctors of Paris who were involved with animal experiments. Having claimed that she had been successful when cursing one of the doctors, who shortly died, she started preparing to work magically on Pasteur. Being uncertain of his appearance she walked through the rain to attend one of his lectures, after which she developed pneumonia and subsequently died. The irony is that the work of Pasteur would have saved her life; the Gods do have a sense of humour.

Sadly, she died a few months before Wescott and Mathers created the Hermetic Order of the Golden Dawn. Had she lived, she would no doubt have played an important part in its creation, and if she had done then it is unlikely that Mathers would have had everything his own way and the order might very have survived. In many respects, this wife of a Shropshire clergyman can be seen as the 'Mother of the Hermetic Order of the Golden Dawn.'

ANNA BONUS KINGSFORD. SHE IS BURIED AT ATCHAM NEAR SHREWSBURY

One cleric of an occult persuasion who is rarely, if ever acknowledged, is a Calvinist Methodist Minister from Montgomery in Mid Wales, John Thomas (1826-1909). He abandoned his ministry when he came into conflict with his superiors concerning both his ability to heal illness and his interest in magnetism.

Subsequently, he began to write under the name Charubel, and his primary work was an occult grimoire entitled *Grimoire Sympathia, The Workshop of the Infinite*. He also ran an occult group, The Celestial Brotherhood, which had members worldwide. One letter which has survived shows how one member came all the way from Bohemia to see him. Three of its members were Alan Leo, who wrote extensively on astrology, John Yarker, influential in the world of Masonry and the creation of the O.T.O., and Major Francis Irwin, who was on good terms with many other occultists of the time and influential in promoting several occult groups. Moving to Frodsham in Cheshire, Charubel produced an occult magazine and wrote a second book on the degrees of the zodiac.

In the archives of the Library of Wales is a small collection of his correspondence and astrological writings. Indeed, in one letter he makes it quite clear how he and his wife Lilly had used their magical prowess against local farmers at Montgomery to adversely affect the weather! Writing in the Western Mail, Arthur Mee quoted from Charubel's account of his life concerning his healing abilities…

> *'It was not long ere I began to try what I could do*
> *Thereby to prove to myself if this new thing was true*
> *My first case was a toothache – the pain was very bad*
> *The man could get no sleep at all, with his head at fever heat*
> *I passed my hand over the spot – I did it with good grace*
> *My fingers glided very slow, but did not touch the face*
> *I threw the pain into the fire, thinking that act the best*
> *The pain must have been consumed*
> *for now, the man had rest.'*

While he was living at Frodsham he produced a number of occult magazines, the most prominent being 'The Psychic Mirror'.

The Psychic Mirror.

THE SEAL OF RHAM

THE REVELATIONS OF NATURE,

BY CHARUBEL.

Charubel's work promoted a healing system without medicine, and by using the spiritual essences of plants, minerals and precious stones he claimed to be able to produce wellness in a variety of complaints. In many respects, this plant grimoire grants easy ingress into the plant and mineral kingdoms. Charubel had received much of his information from the spiritual realms, and the work gave plant sigils, mantras, and their healing properties. He showed in depth how to access their healing potentials, as he considered all plants and minerals to have a consciousness and a soul. Of this, he remarks in his introduction....

> '*I note there is a direct sympathy between the human soul and the soul which pervades and occupies each member, great or small, of the vegetable kingdom.*'

CHARUBEL

Yet Charubel lived most of his life in poverty and was indifferent to this as he considered his healing work to be of utmost importance.

He died aged 82 in 1909.

GRIMOIRE
SYMPATHIA

THE WORKSHOP
OF THE INFINITE:

HEALING WITHOUT MEDICINE USING

THE SPIRITUAL ESSENCE OF PLANTS,

MINERALS AND PRECIOUS STONES.

BY

CHARUBEL

For many people in the occult community, the name of Monica English (1920-79) is perhaps unknown, yet she is a person of great interest.

She appears as Margo in Lois Bourne's account of her life in the world of Gardnerian witchcraft, *'Dancing With Witches,'* where her involvement with a coven in Norfolk is considered. Monica English had her own connections with traditional witchcraft and moved to Shropshire not long after the second world war. Residing near Bishops Castle, in a farmhouse not far from Ratlinghope, she lived with Peter Earle Barnes, some accounts say bigamously.

He was Master of the local Hunt, and the United Hunt is still in existence today. Later they parted company, and she remarried and went to live in Norfolk, at Gayton not far from Swaffham. Whether she created a coven in Shropshire is not known, but she may have had some influence upon one group who had connections with south Shropshire, and who claim to have been founded about the time she lived in the area.

MONICA ENGLISH

In 2003 I came into contact with an individual living not far from me, with their partner, in a remote corner of the Clun Valley. While I'm not revealing their real name, this person wrote and publicised material under the name 'Christos Beest'…. Christ's Beast. Although he was building a following in the locality for his artwork no one knew of his occult connections with the Order of the Nine Angles. Christos Beest told me that he was the 'Outer Head' of this Satanic group. The O.N.A. was legendary, and it was something they liked to promote: no one on the UK occult scene had a good word for them. Their occult mix of Satanism and the swastika went down like the proverbial lead balloon with other occult groups and individuals of various hues. Some of their material has been published on the internet, and those who feel the urge can study it there. But how much is real is another matter.

During my conversations with both Christos Beest and Mrs Christos Beest, they told me how they had been working on various sites in Shropshire. Their preference was for hills which had a quartz stratum in their makeup, as these were considered to be better working sites. Two places they told me they had been performing magical works were Stiperstones and the Caer Caradoc hill south of Clun. Although their brand of magic was not for me, I did take the opportunity to ask them about it and the history of the O.N.A. It became quite clear to me that they were a small group whose members were solitary in nature. Part of 'becoming one of us' required the aspirant to cut themselves off from society and perform a retreat for several weeks.

Mrs Christos Beest told me how she had lived in a tent in the bleak lands of Beacon hill south of Beguildy in Radnorshire as her retreat. Not an easy feat even when the weather is kind. The history of the order was a little vague. I was told that the group had its roots in an earlier occult group which had been created in the early 1950's in the Camlad valley; this is a rural area between Montgomery, Churchstoke and Ratlinghope, and is the area where Monica English was living during the same period.

Seemingly there was a female Satanic group known as the 'Daughters of Baphomet' with the same genesis. Of course, one may wonder how true all this is, and I am not in a position to say one way or the other. I am merely including these conversations of fifteen years ago with one of the prominent members of this community, as a record of what I have been told. At one point, Christos Beest said that during the mid-1980's they had tried setting up a small occult commune on the Longmynd, but it hadn't worked out. I knew of this attempt as I had previously read the adverts for it in the occult magazine '*Lamp of Thoth*', an occult publication of that time, and had wondered who these people were.

However, during the early years of the 1990's the country was gripped in a panic about occult and sexual abuse. Despite the media whipping up a frenzy, as one might expect them to do (after all what editor would let the facts get in the way of a story?), Christos Beest, for some strange reason best known to himself, was visited and interviewed by the Reverend Kevin Logan. This cleric had been in cahoots with the Tory M.P. Geoffrey Dicken, (now deceased) over exposing what became known as Satanic Ritual Abuse, or S.R.A. Dicken had produced a large dossier, or so he claimed, and was going to present it to parliament, but strangely it went missing; that is if it ever existed. He, with others and the press, were feeding the rising panic in society over anything that was of an occult nature.

This literal witch hunt resulted in several families having children removed on flimsy evidence of the parents being pagan, or having occult interests. It also resulted in shops like the world-famous 'Sorcerer's Apprentice' in Leeds being fire-bombed by Christian fanatics, who were applauded by self-righteous bible bashing groups. In fact, for a while it was not a good time to say publicly that you were different. The government did hold its own inquiry into the Satanic panic but concluded there was nothing in it, which was true. However, the groups who created it are still around and occasionally one hears of them and their conferences.

Christos Beest went on to say that the Reverend Logan had told him that he had spoken to the police and they knew where he was going and what time he would be back. Although a bemused Christos Beest told me Logan needn't have bothered as he wouldn't have been invited to stay.

One thing that Christos Beest did produce with his artwork was the Sinister Tarot, a tarot pack which is not widely known. When I last saw the 'Beests' in 2005, Christos had become a Catholic and was off to Scotland to live, while Mrs Christos Beest had gone back to teaching English. No doubt life had caught up with this curious couple.

The O.N.A. are not the only occult group to have a liking for Shropshire and its border country. Many years ago I was reading through Doreen Valiente's work *An ABC of Witchcraft*, where she mentions the story of Nanny Morgan briefly. This intrigued me as I pondered how she, living in Sussex, would have known of an obscure Shropshire story, one which the indigenous population barely knew. Years after this I was in the Witchcraft Museum at Boscastle in Cornwall, where I had an opportunity to speak to the owner, Graham King, about Doreen Valiente and her possible links to Shropshire. I had surmised that she might have heard of Nanny Morgan because of her connections with Roy Bowers, also known as Robert Cochrane, who had developed his own brand of witchcraft in the early 1960's, known as *The Clan of Tubal Cain*.

While there are those today who would claim that Bowers practised a family tradition, this has been challenged by some. Writing some years ago in the occult magazine *The Cauldron*, editor Michael Howard carried a story how the Bowers family knew nothing about the alleged family tradition. Subsequently, there have been those ever since who have taken a differing view and suggested that the individual had gotten their family history wrong. Whatever the truth is, I feel it is irrelevant because quite simply, if Bowers had made up his occult tradition, so what? If it worked, which its adherents claimed it did, who's to say why the Gods had chosen this individual through whom to manifest a new occult current? - despite his flaws, or maybe because of them.

As Bowers had a fondness for caving and was known to have gone to South Wales in his explorations, Shropshire and the Stiperstones was not that far away, particularly with its legends of Wild Edric and his faery wife Godda, to which he could have easily been drawn. And the Stiperstones was also a place favoured by cavers because of the old lead mines under the local hills.

Fortunately, Graham King put me in touch with somebody in Boscastle who could answer this query.

Later that day I met John of Monmouth, the name which he prefers to be known by in public. He confirmed to me that Bowers would have been familiar with the locality and its legends, and that some members of his group, which had carried on after his death, had moved to Shropshire and were working on some of the sites such as the Stiperstones. (Although with the O.N.A. working up there as well it must have got crowded some nights.)

Bowers took his own life at midsummer 1966, aged twenty-eight, from belladonna and tranquillizers. He had done this after his wife had left him, owing to his relationship with a female member of their coven, the group having broken up after this. However, two of its members, Ronald 'Chalky' White and George 'Bang Bang' Stannard (also known as Winter), reformed the group as the Regency to carry on Bowers' legacy. Stannard claimed that he had been in contact with the occult when he lived in Norfolk, and that he had been introduced to someone from the Swaffham area who had witchcraft connections. This is the area where Monica English was domiciled after her Shropshire sojourn. Although I understand that at some point he had taken Gardnerian initiation.

Writing about the Regency in the 1970's occult magazine *Man, Myth and Magic*, Ronald White claimed that it had all been made up. The Regency idea was that everyone was a regent for their inner selves, that centre of being where the Goddess and the God dwell. Although it met to perform seasonal festivals, these were seen as allegorical of life and could be interpreted at various levels. Bowers' view that the mysteries were open to all was an idea embraced in the early days of the Regency. Its ceremonies were public, and a sincere belief was all that was required. There was no oath nor membership fee in its early days as it was an open group. However, things changed in the late 1970's. Some stories claim that they came to the attention of the Home Office over some matter, others that at a gathering in Winchester its members were obliged to swear oaths that others were not happy with. Yet others claim that there was a developing racial element concerning

'Arthur and the Matter of Britain.' Again, this is occult gossip in some quarters.

Whatever the truth was, and this'll depend on who you talk to, the Regency disappeared; they had gone to earth in Shropshire. Was Shropshire a choice because of Bowers, or perhaps another, such as Monica English? Was she known to George Stannard who had become involved with the craft in her Norfolk locality? Perhaps none of these?

Or was it the draw of the Edric story?

During a conversation at his house, John of Monmouth told me that when the Regency had gone to earth in Shropshire they had made use of the Wild Edric myth as part of their workings.

Edric, who was a real person and who had held lands prior to the Norman Conquest in south-west Shropshire, was riding one day in the Clun Forest area on the Welsh border. Riding into a clearing he came upon a group of young women singing and dancing. He rushed in and kidnapped the fairest and rode off with her. Three days later she agreed to marry him and told him that her name was Godda. She added, however, that if he ever mentioned her sisters she would leave him and never return. Time went by and all was well until one day, when in a bad mood, he rebuked her and mentioned her sisters. Immediately she disappeared, and he was distraught. At his death he was reunited with her and they dwell under the Stiperstone hill, from where they sometimes ride forth with their retinue. Tradition claims that Godda rides a white horse and is always dressed in green, while Edric blows the hunting horn and his horsemen gallop past with the hunting dogs. It can be fatal to meet them, so legend tells.

Strangely, Shropshire has its own Wild Hunt myth, one that is barely known yet which is a powerful part of the landscape. Godda, probably pronounced Gotha, as the Welsh spelling *dd* is pronounced as *th*, suggests that she was a Welsh woman. Dancing in the glade with her sisters - perhaps sisters in the arte or family members? It's open to interpretation. However, the horse troop, the hounds, and Godda riding a white horse and dressed in green are quite clearly drawing on timeless myths of the Queen of Elfame, the Lady of the Otherworld.

It's easy to see the appeal of this myth to an occult-minded group, one that is embedded in the landscape and becomes a personification of the powers of the land. Heady stuff.

Sadly, George Stannard died in 1983 and Ronald White in 1998, and whilst they are buried in the same graveyard I do not feel that I am at liberty to say where they are buried.

Why Shropshire and the Welsh March should be such a draw for occult-minded individuals is something that has been speculated on by some. Perhaps it is because of the bloodshed over the years where the English fought the Welsh and then both fought the Normans. Maybe it is the rich landscape and the spirit thereof, powerfully fed on past bloodshed and desires. That it is a powerful and rich landscape, one highly suited to magic, makes it surprising that it has been overlooked by most of the occult community.

However, I am sure there are others who have found their way here and are unknown. I have heard of traditional witches near Hay on Wye. The late Andrew Chumbley of the *Cultus Sabbati* told me of a group of folk magicians in south Shropshire not far from Ludlow. Even Dennis Wheatley, the 'Prince of the Occult Novel', would stay with Joan Grant, (who wrote a couple of books in the 1930's about her previous lives in Egypt), at her mansion near Guilsfield, Welshpool. Although Wheatley always claimed that he had had nothing to do with magic, letters exist between him and Grant, now in the archives of the Liverpool Museum, which clearly show how they were planning to perform Venusian rituals. Were these magical rituals being performed or was this a euphemism for something else?

Today I am aware of several individuals who practice their magic along the border, and at least two alchemical laboratories working both day and night in pursuit of the mystery. There are also, of course, various pagan moots and individuals present and a couple of wiccan covens in existence. And in north Powys there are practitioners of traditional witchcraft both secret and silent. In many ways I was fortunate as a child of fifteen, in 1972, to have somebody move into my small Welsh Border village and teach me something of the arte.

Rosemary Marah Howard Booth had been a member of Alex Sanders' 'Notting Hill set' and had, after an exposure in the Sunday papers, lost her job at a Catholic school where she taught. This had happened when her house was broken into by reporters looking for a story after she had read tarot at the school fete. Perhaps it was fate moving everyone around on the great chess board of life. But I was the one who benefitted greatly, as at a young age I had access to the experience and knowledge of a capable practitioner of the arte. Roz, as she liked to be called, had spent some time working with Sanders' brother-in-law, known as Ray Boggart, who lived in Lancashire and was running a Luciferian coven, before such practices became popular within the 'Trad Witchcraft' culture of the UK.

ROSEMARY MARAH HOWARD BOOTH…. (ROZ)
1932-86
SOMETIME WITCH OF CLUN

At this time, I was becoming more interested in other aspects of magic, such as the grimoire traditions and the work of Israel Regardie. In many ways it had become time to move on as the apprenticeship was shape-shifting into the next stage. Roz was an extremely accomplished witch who could do many of the things that were expected of such a person. And I have personally seen her use ritual and trance work to find a missing person who was sadly dead. Their body being found two days later by the police as described. Having access to a good occult library in my teen years and also having a knowledgeable individual to help me understand what I was being taught is something of which I am immensely appreciative. Sadly, Roz died aged 54 on New Year's Day 1986. In time, as the last member of the Clun coven, I passed on the current to a third person who is running with it, thus severing my tie with that time. This I decided was relevant as I had another magical path to follow and felt I couldn't serve two Masters fully.

However, to show that magic can work and does take place I give finally an account of a Goetia working which I performed during the early part of 2010. This account is already in the public domain so I am giving away no great secret. This was a working to conjure the Goetic spirit Seere into the shewstone to help with the housing problems of two individuals. One was severely disabled and getting nowhere with the local housing association, who weren't particularly interested in their plight. The second individual was homeless after a matrimonial breakdown. After some thought and preparation, it was a standard Goetic conjuration which I performed. In some ways, one could suggest that a sledgehammer was being used to crack a nut. The atmospheres that can build up during conjuration can be quite intense, so much so that you easily feel that anything can happen, and sometimes it does. And this working was no exception. The long conjurations, the barbarous words of power, the half-light and rising incense all lent power to the working. Gazing into the shewstone the scryer said with some concern that the spirit had arrived and that they were now arising out of the shewstone. The scryer was alarmed as the spirit was angry for being disturbed and had its face barely a foot away from the scryer as they snarled at them!

After using the time-honoured formulae for testing the spirit and to bring the working under control the situation calmed down, mercifully. The scryer went on to describe the spirit as a man riding upon a white horse. This was good as this is how the spirit appears, but the scryer had no previous knowledge of the spirit or their appearance. Suddenly the shewstone darkened and great black clouds were rolling in the background. The spirit, sitting astride the horse, now had a great army behind them appearing in long columns rising into the distance. At this point, the spirit was instructed to present a member of their legion to come forth to perform the work that was required. A figure moved to the front who was dressed in deep blues and bearing on their chest the seal of the planet Jupiter which was coloured silver.

This was of great significance as the spirit was associated with Jupiter's sign of Pisces and the last 10 degrees of the sign which was allotted by tradition to the moon, so the colouring certainly accorded well. The spirit agreed to resolve the two problems according to the will of the conjuror and in a set time. The disabled person was to vacate their privately rented property at the end of the week with nowhere to go and, quite clearly, they were desperate. They rang me on the Thursday in a distressed state as the bungalow which they were hoping for had been allocated. I managed to calm down the situation and said I would get back on the case to resolve it. Quietly I was furious with the spirit and wondered about Goetic curses for rebellious spirits. However, for some reason I suggested that they wait until the next day. The next morning they were hysterical with joy, the people had gone to the property and left quite ashen and didn't want to stay, this was after they had arrived with their goods and chattels. They gave no reason and turned the property down. The housing people then suggested to the disabled person that if they could sign for the property that day it was theirs and they could move in the next day. With their own home already packed up, it was no problem.

The second individual's outcome was not so dramatic as the property which they had applied for and was of an attractive appearance was turned down by several people who didn't like the atmosphere. This happened until the individual for whom the working was performed was eventually offered the property, which they still live in.

Thus, magic alive and well upon the borders of England and Wales, and I am sure am sure that if asked, all would agree with me that this is a special place, a sacred landscape, and one that has been en-hallowed by the Gods and by time.

Further Reading

Burne, Charlotte S.....Shropshire Folklore (two volumes)

Leather, Ella Mary...The Folklore of Herefordshire

L'Estrange, Ewen.... Witchcraft and Demonianism

Palmer, Roy ....The Folklore of Radnorshire

.... The Folklore of Shropshire

Suggett, Richard......A History of Magic and Witchcraft in Wales

Thanks to the National Library of Wales with its archives and resources, and also Hereford Museum for help given.

Index

Printed in April 2021
by Rotomail Italia S.p.A., Vignate (MI) - Italy